CLASSIC LIQUEURS

The Art of Making and Cooking with Liqueurs

Cheryl Long and Heather Kibbey

Cover Design by Vicki Crampton
Cover Art by David Nastelle

Revised Editions ©1993 & 1994
Copyright © 1990, Reprinted 1992
By Cheryl Long and Heather Kibbey

Library of Congress Cataloging-in-Publication Data

Long, Cheryl.
Classic liqueurs: the art of making and cooking with liqueurs
by Cheryl Long and Heather Kibbey
p.   cm.
Includes index.
1. Liqueurs.   2. Cookery (Liquors)   I. Kibbey, H.L.   II. Title
TP611.L66   1990   641.2'5--dc20   90-37387
ISBN 0-914667-11-4 : $8.95

Printed in the United States of America

Published by:
Culinary Arts Ltd.
P.O. Box 2157
Lake Oswego, Oregon 97035

Books by Culinary Arts Ltd.:

**Classic Liqueurs: The Art Of Making And Cooking
            With Liqueurs
Easy Microwave Preserving
Gourmet Mustards: How To Make And Cook With Them
Gourmet Vinegars: How To Make And Cook With Them
The Best of ScanFest: An authentic treasury of Scandinavian
            recipes and proverbs.**

Publisher's Catalog available upon request.

TABLE OF CONTENTS

ABOUT THE AUTHORS

Cheryl Long, a home economist, is the former Editor of *Restaurateur Magazine* and President of Culinary Arts Ltd. She has authored several books, **How to Make Danish Fruit Liqueurs** and **Easy Microwave Preserving**, and co-authored **How To Make A World Of Liqueurs**. Long formerly edited a microwave magazine, was a food consultant, columnist, and is a free-lance writer and instructor.

Heather Kibbey is the owner of the Northwest Publishers Consortium and Panoply Press, Inc. and has hosted a weekly radio show, *HOUSE CALLS*. She has authored several real estate books such as **First Home Buying Guide**, and was the co-author of **How To Make A World Of Liqueurs**. Kibbey was formerly a magazine editor, food columnist, and is a free-lance writer.

The authors give cooking classes on their favorite culinary subjects as time permits and are currently working on new books. Both authors live with their families in Lake Oswego, Oregon.

INTRODUCTION

Classic Liqueurs came about because of the success of **How To Make A World Of Liqueurs** and **How To Make Danish Fruit Liqueurs,** our two previous books on the subject of home liqueur making. Simply, you enjoyed them and wanted more. The two of us, as friends and fellow food writers, decided to continue our fun-filled challenge. It was!

It is with a real sense of accomplishment that we present our most extensive work ,with liqueur recipes that come as close to duplicating the"classic" ones as the limitations of a home kitchen will allow. Most are so close that we suggest a blindfold test of manufactured liqueurs versus our counterparts. Put them in your best decanters and serve or "gift" them with pride.

Our most creative selves came forth on the food and beverage recipes. We wanted recipes that were truly worth making and remembering–recipes that would not be the same without the liqueurs they were designed for. We enjoyed making them almost as much as our testers enjoyed evaluating them. As usual, we did our share of the tastings too, each dutifully gaining five pounds in the process! Naming each recipe was much like naming our first-born child.

We thoroughly enjoyed the research and want to thank you, our readers and students, for requesting **Classic Liqueurs**.

A Distinguished Tradition

Welcome to a noble and distinguished tradition, that of liqueur making. History credits Hippocrates (400 B.C.) as the first to develop the art of distilling water and aromatic liquids, forerunners of todays liqueurs. In 900 A.D. the first recorded making of alcoholic beverages was by the Arabs and European monks and alchemists in Northern Europe.

Arnáu de Valanova, a 13th century Spanish physician and chemist was the first writer and creator of herbal liqueurs. His liqueurs were so famous that the Pope used them. Liqueurs gained popularity during the 14th century and were thought to prevent the Black Death.

Catherine De Médici lived in 15th century Italy, which was noted as a leading center of liqueur making. Her chefs imported their recipes to France, thus spreading their popularity.

By the 17th and 18th century French liqueur had become a prized and traditional beverage in the English courts. Liqueur-making spread out into the world, utilizing native plants, fruits, liqueurs and flavorings; many prized recipes became the basis for businesses that continue to this day.

BASICS OF LIQUEUR MAKING

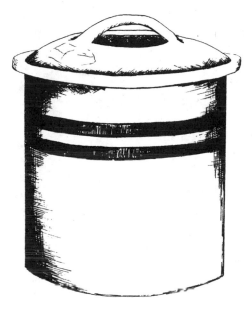

BASICS OF LIQUEUR MAKING

EQUIPMENT
Making liqueurs at home does not require anything really 'special' in the way of equipment. You will need some, but not all of the following:

Aging Containers:
Glass jars with lids (wide mouth, 1-quart or larger are best)
Ceramic crock with lid
Ceramic bowls, glass bottles and/or decanters with either
  screw-on lids/caps or cork/glass caps

Strainers:
Metal colander
Fine wire-mesh strainer
Cloth jelly-bag
White/natural cotton muslin or linen cloth
Cheesecloth
Paper coffee filters

Miscellaneous:
Wooden spoon
Glass or metal measuring cups
Metal measuring spoons
Metal funnel

PREPARATION OF EQUIPMENT

The aging containers should be properly cleaned before use. First, wash them thoroughly with a mixture of baking soda and water (about 4 tablespoons per dishpan). The containers should be sterilized by either boiling them in water for 15 minutes or putting them through a full dishwasher cycle without any detergent.

TYPES OF EQUIPMENT

Kitchen utensils used for liqueur making, such as measuring cups, funnels, etc. should not be made of plastic. (Plastic can impart an "off" flavor to liqueurs.) Metal, ceramic or glass are preferred.

Straining is one of the most important steps in obtaining a clear, quality liqueur. A large-holed metal colander will strain large pieces but you will need finer straining material for smaller pieces and for your last fine straining. If cheesecloth is used, you will need several thicknesses, which can be discarded after use.

The most efficient fine straining is done with either a cloth jelly-bag or with a clean cotton or linen cloth laid inside a strainer. These clothes may be washed and reused. Some prefer to use disposable paper coffee filters for this step, however they are too dense for some of the thicker liqueurs in this book. We recommend that you test a small amount first if you wish to use this method. Try various strainers to see which you prefer.

BOTTLES AND DECANTERS

You will need an assortment of clean bottles or decanters to hold the finished product. For home storage, wine bottles with metal screw-on tops are frequently the most practical container.

For gift giving, small unusual glass bottles with a metal screw-on top, such as condiment, vinegar and small wine bottles, are excellent. Many interesting bottles also can be found in kitchen, glass, gourmet, herb and wine-making shops.

Glass decanters are elegant containers in which to serve or give your special liqueurs. Good places to find inexpensive decanters are garage or rummage sales and second-hand or thrift shops.

Decanters frequently have glass tops with a cork insert. This is fine as long as the cork is clean.

Containers which have held something other than a food or beverage can be difficult to clean and may transfer an offensive or dangerous taste to your liqueur. Therefore, their use is not recommended.

Plastic containers should not be used when making or storing liqueurs. It is also best to avoid all plastic or plastic-lined caps. The flavor from the plastic can be transferred to the liqueur. An occasional exception is when plastic wrap is laid across a bowl in the early stages or to shield an uncoated metal lid from corroding. For example, canning jar lids are usually coated inside; mayonnaise jar lids are not. Plastic wrap may be used if it does not touch the liqueur for the latter.

Cork may be used if you wish, but remember that corks allow evaporation. You may wish to seal the cork with wax or foil to avoid this.

INGREDIENTS

When making any recipe, remember that it is the quality of the ingredients used that determines the final result. There are three main types of ingredients to consider in liqueur making. They are: alcohol, flavorings and water.

Alcohol:

There are a number of types of alcohol bases used in liqueur making. The two most frequently used are 180 to 190 proof pure grain alcohol and 80 proof vodka. Both are easily obtained at your local liquor store.

Pure grain alcohol is a neutral spirit which will be diluted half-and-half with water. It has no taste of its own to interfere with the liqueur flavorings. When purchasing a pure grain alcohol, know that all brands are equal.

Vodka, like pure grain alcohol, is a neutral spirit usually made from distilled grains and is an ideal base in liqueur making . There are differences from brand to brand. The purifying and refining processes of the distiller determine the end quality.

Good vodka should be colorless, odorless, and have no real taste of its own. Take time to find the 'smoothest' vodka in your price range.We prefer 80 proof over 100 proof.

The other alcohol bases used in liqueur making are brandy, cognac, American or Irish whiskey, scotch and rum. These all have pronounced tastes of their own and are frequently used with vodka or pure grain alcohol to add their special flavor. Choose them with care and use them sparingly.

Basic brandy is distilled from fermented grape juices. Some brandies are made from other fruits. Avoid fruit-flavored brandies in liqueur making, as they will compete with your flavorings. Choose a good-tasting brandy but avoid the rare, aged and costly brandies which should be enjoyed on their own.

Cognac is a very fine French brandy which derives its name from the area where the wine grapes it is made from are grown, Cognac, France. You may, of course, substitute any brandy for cognac, but when we recommend cognac it is for a superior liqueur.

Whiskey, or 'whisky'as the Scotch and Canadian versions are spelled, is almost as varied in taste as rum. American whiskey is generally distilled from rye, wheat or corn. Irish whiskey and Scotch (short for Scottish Whisky) are usually made from malted barley. We have found it best to use Irish whiskey in a traditionally Irish liqueur such as Irish Cream, for more authentic flavor. Wherever this is important, we have indicated it; if not indicated, use a whiskey that is pleasing to your taste.

Rums are distilled from sugar and molasses. Most are made in tropical countries where the sugarcane grows, most notably the Caribbean. The lighter-colored, lighter-bodied Puerto Rican or Barbados rums work well. The Jamaican rums are heavier and sweeter. Take care to match the rum to the type of liqueur. Our best advice is to choose a rum that you find smooth and pleasing.

FRUITS, FLAVORINGS & OTHER INGREDIENTS

Fresh fruits are the most delicate ingredients in liqueur making. It does make a difference whether the fruits are picked at the peak of their season or are the last stragglers. There really is no substitute, but try to follow the fresh fruit seasons if you can.

Fruit peel, often referred to as zest, should be thinly cut, away from the white portion of the fruit. Citrus fruits should be washed very carefully to remove dust and chemical sprays. Liqueurs can be ruined by a mold, spoilage or spray that is present in the fruit.

Dried fruit liqueurs can be made any time of the year. But again, choose fresh quality dried fruits for best taste. Dried fruits can deteriorate with age, but it is a slower process.

Fresh seeds, herbs and spices are frequently called for in our liqueur recipes. Always purchase the freshest and best quality spices, etc. possible. While the more common varieties are available in a supermarket, others such as dried angelica root may not be. Health food stores and herb/spice shops usually carry a wider selection at more economical prices.

In order to release the full flavor of a fruit or seed, the recipe will indicate that it be cut open or 'bruised.' A mortar and pestle are ideal for bruising; however, a small bowl and the back of a spoon may be substituted. Bruising is a partial crushing of the seed to release the inner flavor to the liquid medium.

Pure glycerine is an odorless, colorless, syrupy liquid prepared by the hydrolysis of fats and oils. It is used as a food preservative and is available at drug stores, liqueur and winemaking shops, and some herb stores. We think of it as a 'smoother.' It performs two services: first, it gives additional body to thinner liqueurs that do not have as much natural body as desired. Secondly, it adds a smoothness and slipperiness in the tasting or sipping of a liqueur that gives a professional quality. In general, quantities of glycerine will vary, depending upon the need of the individual liqueur. However, we recommend that you do not exceed 1 tablespoon per quart of liqueur.

Glucose syrup is a sweet syrup that can be found in cake decorating shops. It has the consistency of corn syrup, and in its commercial form often contains dextrin and maltose. It is not as sweet as the sugar and water combinations that we use in our recipes, but is an interesting alternative if you wish to experiment. It has the advantage of having a thick consistency which makes the addition of glycerine unnecessary.

WATER

Water quality and taste vary considerably from one area to another. If you have good-tasting drinking water, you may choose to use it in liqueur making. However, for the best quality control in liqueur making, use distilled water. Distilled water will not impart any off flavors and you will receive the fullest taste from your liqueur.

AGING

There is one element in liqueur making that is absolutely essential to good quality and taste: the aging process. We are amazed to find that so many recipes we have seen ignore this step. Aging removes the raw edge of the alcohol, no matter which type of alcohol is used. It lends mellowness and a professional quality to a liqueur that develops only with time. Your homemade liqueur will be quite different from its commercial counterpart if not correctly aged.

We have indicated minimum aging times for each recipe. After this period of time, the liqueur is certainly ready for cooking purposes, but you may choose to age it additionally before drinking. We recommend a taste test at this time. Except for the refrigerated cream liqueurs, which should be used within 6 months, most of our recipes will be at their peak after 1 year's aging. Non-cream liqueurs stay at their peak for about 3 years.

If you choose to double, triple or halve a liqueur recipe, it will not affect the aging time.

SIPHONING

Before the initial straining, most liqueurs have particles of fruit or spices suspended throughout the liquid medium. Careful straining will eliminate these. During aging, some liqueurs form a layer of clear, particle-free liquid and a second, cloudy layer. Attempts to strain this merely result in recombining the two layers, producing a cloudy liquid. Siphoning is a much more efficient way to solve this problem.

Use a piece of plastic tubing 20 to 24 inches long. (Beer and winemaking stores carry tubes especially for this purpose.) Place one end of the tube in the bottle of liqueur so that the end is at a level 1/2 inch above the sediment. Bend the tube and suck gently on the other end until the liqueur fills the tube. With your finger over that end, place it in the empty bottle and at the same time, raise the bottle of liqueur so that the layer of sediment is 4 inches or so above the empty bottle. To stop the flow, just lower the full bottle so that the liquid levels in both bottles are the same. When the clear liquid has been siphoned off, discard the sediment.

BRAND NAMES

As you leaf through the recipe section of this book you may find that some of your favorite liqueurs seem to be missing. For instance, you will not see a recipe labeled 'Galliano' because Galliano is the brand name for the specific commercially pro-duced liqueur. Legally, we may not use these brand names for our liqueur counterparts, and so we have invented our own names. (Our facsimile of Galliano is called 'Italian Gold Liqueur', for instance.)

Some names, such as Amaretto and Irish Cream are not brand names, even though we may associate them with one major producer. For these liqueurs, we were legally permitted to use the familiar title.

EQUIVALENT LIQUID MEASURES

1 teaspoon	=	6 dashes
3 teaspoons	=	1 tablespoon
2 tablespoons	=	1 ounce
5 ⅓ tablespoons	=	⅓ cup
8 ounces	=	1 cup
16 tablespoons	=	1 cup
2 cups	=	1 pint
16 ounces	=	1 pint
2 pints	=	1 quart
25.6 ounces	=	⅕ gallon or ⅘ quart (known as a 'fifth')
32 ounces	=	1 quart
4 quarts	=	1 gallon
5 fifths	=	1 gallon
1 pony	=	1 ounce
1 jigger	=	1 ½ ounces
1 dash	=	less than ⅛ teaspoon

ABBREVIATIONS USED

oz.	=	ounce
tsp.	=	teaspoon
Tbsp.	=	tablespoon
lb.	=	pound
pt.	=	pint
qt.	−	quart

METRIC CONVERSION

1 milliliter	=	.034 fluid ounces
1 liter	=	33.8 fluid ounces or 4.2 cups
1 fluid ounce	=	29.56 milliliters
1 fluid cup	=	236 milliliters
1 fluid quart	=	946 milliliters
1 teaspoon	=	5 milliliters
1 tablespoon	=	15 milliliters

MAKING FRUIT LIQUEURS

MAKING LIQUEURS

The making of cordials, liqueurs or ratifia immigrated to America with its earliest settlers. Family recipes were brought to the New World and carefully guarded. Some recipes for fine liqueurs were designed for formal dining and special occasions. Other recipes were for 'medicinal cordials'.

Fruits, herbs and spices were common ingredients for early liqueurs. The settlers found that they had to make substitutions for ingredients not found in the New World. But in substituting discovered that many new native fruits were extremely good for liqueur-making.

Gracious hospitality dictated that guests be greeted with a small glass of sweet liqueur, no matter what time of day they arrived. Liqueurs were also a relaxing touch served with tea or coffee after dinner. Often the after-dinner liqueurs were called 'digestive cordials'.

The custom of using liqueurs in mixed drinks was not popular until this century. It began in the Prohibition days when smooth, sweet tasting liqueurs softened rough 'bathtub' gin. Later, noted liqueur companies and distillers developed recipes that became widely popular.

APPLE LIQUEUR

Our version of Applejack

Apple liqueur has been made in Germany since the 1700's. Different varieties of apples may be used; each gives its own unique flavor. **Apple liqueur** *is flavorful and versatile in cooking; add to apple or mince pies for unexpected richness. Ready in 2 months. Makes over 1 quart.*

2 1/2 lbs. sweet apples*
2 cups vodka
2 cups brandy
1 1/2 cups granulated sugar
3/4 cup water

Wash apples and remove stems. Cut into wedges or slices and put into aging container. Pour vodka and brandy over apples, stirring with a wooden spoon. Cap and age in a cool place for 1 month.

Pour liqueur mixture through a fine cloth bag that has been placed into a large bowl. Set bag with apples into another bowl to drain. Clean aging container, removing any sediment. Pour strained liqueur back into clean aging container. Twist top of bag and with the back of a spoon press out any liqueur possible. (Some apples are soft and easy to press, others are hard and don't permit much liquid to be pressed out.) Pour liqueur/juice into aging container.

Combine sugar and water in a small saucepan. Heat, bringing up to a boil, stir constantly. Set aside to cool. Pour strained liqueur and cooled sugar-water into aging container. Cap container and let age at least 1 more month. Liqueur improves with additional aging.

After aging time, check clarity. If any additional straining is needed, do it at this time. A fine wire mesh, cloth or coffee-filter is best for finer straining. When desired clarity is reached, bottle and store in a cool, dark place.

*Variation: Tart Apple Liqueur is crisp and refreshing. Increase the sugar to 2 cups and follow recipe and directions.

Variation: Spiced Apple Liqueur is made by adding two 3" cinnamon sticks and 10 whole cloves. Remove spices before pressing liquid from apples. Both sweet and tart apples are good.

Variation: Our version of **Calvados**, a famous French apple liqueur, may be simulated by substituting a good French brandy.

Variation: Quince liqueur can be made quite simply by substituting the apple-like quince fruit for the apples.

APRICOT LIQUEUR

Capture fresh apricots at the peak of the season and make a smooth and fragrant liqueur. Lovely color and taste make it a favorite. Ready in 1 to 2 months. Makes about 1 quart.

1 1/2 lbs., (about 3 cups), pitted fresh apricots
1 fifth vodka
2 cups granulated sugar
1/2 cup water

Place cut apricots and vodka in aging container; set aside. Place sugar and water in a small saucepan. Heat over medium heat, stirring constantly until sugar is dissolved. Remove from heat and let cool. When cool, pour sugar liquid into aging container. Stir gently to combine. Cap and place in a cool, dark place. Stir weekly with a wooden spoon for 1 month.

Put a colander into a large mixing bowl. Pour apricot mixture into colander. Remove fruit; may be saved and used as liqueured fruit if desired. Pour liqueur through finer strainer, or unbleached muslin cloth. Discard fine particles. Re-strain until clear. Re-bottle and label as desired. Liqueur is ready but improves with additional months aging.

Variation: Rock Candy Apricot Liqueur is made by substituting 1 lb. of clear rock candy for the granulated sugar and water in Apricot recipe. Omit heating. Place candy in aging container with apricots and vodka. Continue as directed. Stir weekly until rock candy has completely dissolved. Proceed as directed.

DRIED APRICOT LIQUEUR

*When fresh apricots aren't available you can still make **Apricot Liqueur**. Dried apricots are excellent as a liqueur base. You get a bonus with the plumped, liqueured apricots after making liqueur. Use them in desserts, compotes, or stuff a pork roast with a mixture of apples, prunes and the liqueured apricots for a special Scandinavian treat. Ready in 1 to 2 months. Makes about 1 quart.*

1 lb. dried apricots
1 fifth vodka
2 cups granulated sugar
1/2 cup water

Cut apricots in half . Place apricots and vodka into aging container; set aside. Place sugar and water in a small saucepan. Heat over medium heat, stirring constantly until sugar has completely dissolved. Remove from heat and let cool. When cool, pour sugar liquid into aging container. Stir to combine. Seal and place in a cool, dark place. Stir weekly with a wooden spoon for 1 month. Taste and evaluate aging at this time. If more time is needed allow 2 to 4 more weeks.

Place a colander or large strainer in a large mixing bowl. Pour dried apricot mixture through colander. Remove dried apricots, which are now plumped and liqueured. (These can now be used in a variety of recipes or eaten as is.) Pour liqueur through finer strainer or unbleached muslin cloth. Repeat as needed until clear. Bottle and label as desired. Liqueur is ready but improves with additional aging.

BANANA LIQUEUR

A tropical liqueur that has many uses. Excellent in punches as well as a special ingredient in any banana cake recipe. Substitute rum if you wish a more tropical taste. Ready in 2 1/2 months. Makes a little over 1 fifth.

1 large just ripe banana, peeled
1 fifth vodka **or** light rum
1 1/4 cups granulated sugar
1/2 cup water
2" piece of vanilla bean

Mash banana. Place in a large jar, bowl or crock. Pour vodka over mashed banana. With a wooden spoon push banana below the surface of vodka. (The banana will turn dark brown quickly if exposed to the air.) Cover well to prevent evaporation. Let stand for 2 weeks. Pour through a wire strainer to remove larger pieces of banana. Discard banana.

Combine water and sugar and heat in a saucepan* to dissolve sugar, stir constantly. When dissolved, set aside to cool. Re-strain liqueur through fine cloth (linen, muslin or triple cheese-cloth). Strain again as necessary until liqueur is clear.

Add cooled sugar water to strained liqueur. Add a 2-inch piece of vanilla bean that has been slit open. Stir with wooden spoon. Put into jar, bottle or crock and cover well. Let age 1 month, then remove vanilla bean. Do final straining as before, if necessary for clarity. Pour liqueur into bottle(s) and cap. Let age 1 more month before serving.

Note: Can be used without last month's aging if used for cooking or in punches.

***Microwave Directions:** Combine sugar and water in a medium microwave-safe bowl or 4-cup glass measure. Stir to combine. Microwave on **HIGH (100%)** power for 45 seconds; stir and microwave for 30 seconds more; stir again. Set aside to cool and continue as directed.

BLACK CURRANT LIQUEUR

Our Version of Crème De Cassis

This spiced dried fruit liqueur is similar to **Crème De Cassis**. *A classic ingredient in many gourmet recipes. Keep an extra bottle for cooking. Ready in 4 months. Makes about 1 1/2 pints.*

1 1/2 cups dried black currants
1 cup granulated sugar
2 cups brandy
1 cinnamon stick
3 whole allspice
6 whole cloves

Combine all ingredients, except sugar, in aging container. Stir with wooden spoon to combine. Cover or cap tightly and let age for 2 months in a cool, dark place. After initial aging, strain off fruit and spices using a colander or wire mesh strainer. Set drained fruit aside.* Pour liqueur back into cleaned aging container, add sugar. Stir well with wooden spoon to dissolve sugar. Recap and age at least 2 more months. Shake or stir once in awhile to assist sugar in dissolving. Re-strain through fine strainer or cloth jelly bag to remove any small particles of fruit or spices. When clear, re-bottle and seal. Ready in 2 1/2 months.

*Tip: Remove spices, refrigerate fruit. The fruit may be used in cooking, excellent in mince pies.

BLUEBERRY LIQUEUR

A wonderful liqueur that can be made with either fresh or frozen blueberries. This becomes a rich deep-blue colored liqueur. Ready in 3 months. Makes over 1 quart.

4 cups blueberries, rinsed and drained
1 1/2 cups pure grain alcohol*
1 1/2 cups water*
1 cup water
1 1/2 cups granulated sugar
2 thin strips lemon peel

23

Place berries in aging container and mash with the back of a wooden spoon (or an old-fashioned potato masher works very well). Add alcohol and the 1 1/2 cups of water to the berries, stirring to combine. Cover container with lid or plastic wrap and let stand at room temperature or cooler for 2 weeks. Stir every few days.

Tip: If weather is very warm, berry mixture may be put in the refrigerator.

After initial aging, strain mixture over a large bowl through a colander or coarse wire mesh strainer. Discard fruit residue. Clean out aging container to remove all sediment.

Bring 1 cup water to a boil and pour over sugar and lemon peel. Stir well to completely dissolve sugar. Let cool to room temperature. Remove lemon peel and discard. Pour cooled sugar-water mixture into aging container, add strained blueberry liquid. Stir to combine. Cap and let age 1 1/2 months more.

After second aging, strain mixture again through fine strainer, wire or cloth, to remove all sediment. Re-strain as needed until clarity is reached. Bottle and cap as desired. May be used now for cooking but for serving as a liqueur age at least 1 more month, improves with additional time.

*****Variation:** 3 cups 80-proof vodka may be substituted for the pure grain alcohol and the water if desired.

Variation: Spiced Blueberry Liqueur is easily made by adding 1/2 teaspoon whole cloves and 1/2 teaspoon whole coriander to the Blueberry Liqueur recipe.

CHERRY LIQUEUR

Our version of Cherry Heering

*This recipe is exceptionally close to the classic ruby-red **Cherry Heering Liqueur** from Denmark. Use dark Bing, or other sweet red cherries for the best flavor and color. You may vary the hint of almond taste by how you handle the cherry pits (see variation). Easy to make. Ready in 3 months. Makes about 1 quart.*

1 1/2 lbs. red cherries, with pits, no stems
1 1/2 to 2 cups granulated sugar (sweetness to taste)
2 1/2 cups vodka
1 cup brandy

Mix vodka, brandy and sugar in a large glass measure or medium mixing bowl. Stir well to dissolve. Cut each washed cherry slightly to open, leave in pits. Place cherries in 2 sterile, quart wide mouth jars or 1 larger aging container. Pour liquid mixture over cherries, stir and cap with tight lids. For the first two weeks shake jars several times. Let age in a cool, dark place. Age 3 months, minimum, for best flavor. Strain off liqueur through wire mesh strainer, discard cherries. Re-bottle as desired.

Variation: Almond-Cherry - For a more prominent 'almond' flavor, pit all or part of the cherries. Place cherry pits in a clean cloth and hit with a hammer to break them up slightly. Put broken pits and pitted cherries in jars or large container and continue as directed.

Variation: "Sugarless Cherry" - Substitute 1 cup (8 oz.) apple juice concentrate, undiluted for the 1 1/2 to 2 cups of sugar in this recipe. Proceed as directed. The 'sugars' present will be natural fruit sugars rather than the granulated processed sugars. Taste is excellent; aging is the same.

ROYAL ANNE CHERRY LIQUEUR

While all varieties of cherries can be made into a liqueur, there are differences in flavor, color and sweetness which require recipe adjustments for best results. This recipe is one of the most outstanding variations developed. It has a fresh natural flavor and the exquisite color can best be compared to a golden sunset. Ready in 3 months. Makes about 1 quart.

1 1/2 lbs. fresh Royal Anne cherries, with pits, no stems
1 1/2 cups granulated sugar
2 1/2 cups vodka
1 cup brandy

Wash cherries. Cut each cherry with a knife to open up. Place cherries in aging container. Pour sugar over cherries, stir with wooden spoon to mix well. Pour vodka and brandy over cherry mixture. Stir well to combine and partly dissolve sugar. Cover container and place in a cool place. Stir regularly in the first month to assist sugar in dissolving. Cap and place in a cool, dark place for 2 more months.

After aging, pour liqueur through colander which has been placed in a large mixing bowl. Discard cherries. Strain again through fine wire mesh or cloth until desired clarity is reached. Bottle as desired. May be served immediately but improves with additional aging.

CRANBERRY LIQUEUR

Our version of Cranberria and Finnish Karp

A liqueur of magnificent color and taste. It will become a Holiday tradition for serving and gift giving. Excellent in punches and cooking. Fresh or whole frozen cranberries may be used in this recipe. Ready in 5 1/2 months. Makes about 1 fifth.

4 cups (one 12-ounce bag) cranberries
1 cup pure grain alcohol* and
1 cup water*
2 to 2 1/2 cups granulated sugar
1/2 cup water

Rinse and check cranberries. Discard soft or spoiled cranberries. Remove any stems. Chop very coarsely. (A food processor does this quickly and easily.) Place chopped cranberries in aging container(s). Pour sugar over cranberries; pour liquids in next. Stir well with a wooden spoon. Cap and store in a cool, dark place. Stir once a week for 2 weeks. Let age 8 weeks longer.

After initial aging, strain through metal colander. Discard cranberries. Return liqueur to aging container. Let age 3 months longer. Re-strain through fine strainer or cloth to remove any particles or seeds from cranberries. Bottle as desired.

*Variation: 2 cups rum or 80-proof vodka may be substituted for the pure grain alcohol and the 1 cup water in this recipe.

Variation: "Sugarless" Cranberry Liqueur - Substitute 1 cup (8 oz.) apple juice concentrate for the 2 to 2 1/2 cups granulated sugar in this recipe. Proceed as directed. The sugars present will be the natural fruit sugars rather than the processed granulated sugars. Taste will be slightly more on the tart side but excellent overall. Aging is decreased by 1 month.

CRÈME DE PRUNELLE LIQUEUR

This liqueur is our reproduction of a French liqueur that is made from a variety of a wild purple plum known as prunelle. While we thought that it would be a good liqueur, we were surprised that it turned out to be a great liqueur. Any variety of dried prunes may be used in this recipe. We have noted subtle differences in the liqueur depending upon the flavor, sweetness and quality of the prunes used. Excellent in meat recipes, especially pork, as well as for sipping. May be made at any time of year. Ready in 3 months. Makes about 1 quart.

1 1/2 lbs. dried pitted prunes, cut into halves
1 1/2 cups granulated sugar
2 1/4 cups vodka
1 1/2 cups brandy

Place cut prunes in aging container. Add sugar, vodka and brandy; stirring well to combine. Cap and place in a cool place for one month. Stir weekly to dissolve sugar.

After initial aging, pour liquid through a wire strainer placed over a large mixing bowl. Press liqueur juices from prunes with the back of a wooden spoon. Remove prunes from liqueur. Prunes may be saved for cooking. Re-strain liqueur using finer straining material until desired clarity is reached. Bottle as desired. Age 2 more months for best flavor before serving.

Variation: Spiced Crème De Prunelle is an easy variation of this French favorite. Just add a 3" cinnamon stick and 8 whole allspice to the initial ingredients. Let age as directed and remove spices at first straining. Proceed as directed.

ELDERBERRY LIQUEUR

Elderberries make an old-fashioned and memorable liqueur. Fresh berries are best. Follow directions as for **Blueberry Liqueur**. See page 23. Three cups of 80-proof vodka may be substituted for the 1 1/2 cups pure grain alcohol and the 1 1/2 cups water if desired.

ENGLISH DAMSON PLUM LIQUEUR

No English kitchen would be without Damson plums. They are eaten fresh or put into jams, conserves and full-bodied English liqueurs. Agatha Christie's "Miss Marple" serves up this tradition for her favorite guests. We are certain that Miss Marple would approve of and appreciate this recipe. The liqueur is perfect in Trifle recipes too. Ready in 4 months. Makes about 1 quart.

2 1/2 lbs. Damson plums, washed, pitted and halved
1 1/2 cups granulated sugar
1 cup pure grain alcohol*
1 cup water
2/3 cup brandy

Place prepared plums in a large aging container. Sprinkle sugar over plums and mix gently with a wooden spoon. Pour alcohol, water and brandy over mixture; stir gently. Cap and place in a cool, dark place. Stir regularly for the first month, or until sugar is dissolved.

After sugar is dissolved, strain mixture through a colander placed over a large mixing bowl. With the back of a wooden spoon, press out juice from plums. Plums may be discarded or saved for a cooking use if desired. Re-strain liqueur through fine wire mesh or cloth until desired clarity is reached. Re-bottle as desired. Best if aged an additional month before serving.

* Note: 80 proof vodka may be substituted for pure grain alcohol if desired. However, increase amount to 2 cups vodka and eliminate the 1 cup water from recipe.

HAWAIIAN FRUIT LIQUEUR

The tropical islands of Hawaii boast huge pineapple plantations. Sweet, juicy pineapples blended with ripe bananas and laced with Hawaiian rum form the basis for this truly luscious liqueur. You will find it a versatile performer in any mixed drinks, punches and foods. Ready in 2 months. Makes over 1 quart.

3 large bananas, peeled
2 cups fresh-cooked or canned pineapple chunks in
        unsweetened juice; drain and reserve juice
1 fifth light rum
1 1/4 cups granulated sugar
1 cup pineapple juice (reserved)
3" piece vanilla bean
6 drops yellow food coloring

Mash banana. Quickly combine banana, pineapple chunks and rum in an aging container.

In small saucepan, combine sugar, reserved juice and vanilla bean. Bring to a boil. Boil for 1 minute, stirring constantly. Cool to lukewarm. Add the sugar syrup to the fruit and rum mixture; stir to mix well. Cover and let stand in a cool, dark place for 1 month, stirring at least once a week.

After initial aging, strain through colander into a large bowl. Press fruit with potato masher or back of wooden spoon to obtain juice. Discard the fruit and vanilla bean. Re-strain the liqueur several times, using progressively finer filtering material until maximum clarity is achieved. Return to aging container or bottle. Add food coloring; mix well. Age for 1 month, minimum, before serving. If sediments form at bottom of bottle, re-strain and re-bottle.

HUCKLEBERRY LIQUEUR

Huckleberries make a wonderful, slightly tart liqueur. Pick enough on a summer outing to make this recipe. Follow directions as for **Blueberry Liqueur**. See page 23.

LEMON LIQUEUR

Our version of Dopio Cedro

This is one of our personal favorites. Refreshing lemon liqueur is excellent to sip, a natural in punches and many cocktails and superb in cooking and baking. Reminisant of a wonderful Italian lemon liqueur called **Dopio Cedro**. *Makes about 1 fifth.*

2 large lemons
water as needed
2 cups granulated sugar
2 cups vodka

Rinse lemons and pat dry. Thinly peel zest (thin outer layer) strips from lemons. Do not include whiter inner peel. Place zest strips into medium saucepan. Cut lemons in half and squeeze juice into measuring cup. Remove any seeds. Measure juice and add enough water to bring to the 1 cup mark. Pour lemon juice mixture into saucepan with zest, add sugar and stir. Bring mixture to a boil, stirring frequently. When it reaches a boil, reduce heat and simmer for 10 minutes. Remove from heat and cool.

Pour lemon mixture into aging container, add vodka and stir. Cap and age for 4 weeks in a cool, dark place.

After initial aging, pour through metal strainer into bowl to remove zest. Lemon peel may be saved for use in cooking, if desired. Pour liqueur back into cleaned aging container for an additional month of aging.

When aging is completed, strain liqueur through fine cloth (such as muslin) which is placed over a large bowl. Repeat as needed. A cloudy layer may form on top even after several strainings. The cloudy portion may be poured off and reserved for cooking if desired. Bottle and cap as desired. Liqueur is now ready to be used in cooking but is better for drinking after an additional 3 month's aging.

OLD FASHIONED DRIED FRUIT LIQUEUR

"Simple to make and simply delicious" best describes this wonderful liqueur. It offers a bonus of liqueured fruits that are plumped, brandied and ready for topping ice cream, frozen yogurt, pound cake or your favorite dessert creation. Most dried fruits may be used in this recipe; our favorites are apricots, peaches, pears, pineapple, and prunes. Ready in 1 month. Makes about 1 fifth.

1 lb. dried fruit of choice
1 bottle (750 ml.) **or** 3 1/3 cups dry white wine
1 cup brandy
1 1/2 cups granulated sugar
1/2 cup water

Place dried fruit, wine and brandy in aging container. Stir gently. Cover and set aside.

Combine sugar and water in small saucepan. Heat gently, stirring constantly. Remove from heat when sugar has dissolved. Let cool. Add cooled sugar mixture to dried fruit mixture; stirring to combine. Re-cover and place in a cool place for 1 month, stirring occasionally.

After aging, strain off fruit by pouring mixture through a metal colander that has been placed over a large bowl. Save fruit for serving. Re-strain liqueur through fine wire strainer or cloth to remove fine particles. Strain until desired clarity is reached. Bottle as desired.

ORANGE LIQUEUR

A fresh, natural tasting liqueur that is excellent for cooking and baking. Especially good with chocolate. May be used when young for cooking and baking but best for sipping with full aging time. Ready in 3 to 6 months. Makes over 1 quart.

4 large, sweet oranges
  water as needed
1 1/2 to 2 cups granulated sugar
1 cup pure grain alcohol, (180-190 proof)*, mixed with
1 cup water

Rinse oranges and pat dry. Thinly peel zest (thin outer orange skin) from one orange. (Do not peel into the white part of the orange skin, as it is bitter.) Cut up peel into small strips and place in a medium saucepan.** Cut all oranges in half (including the one that has been peeled.) Squeeze juice into a 2-cup measure, add water if needed to bring up to that mark. Pour 2 cups juice into saucepan with zest; add sugar and stir. Bring up to a boil, stirring frequently. Immediately reduce heat and simmer for 10 to 12 minutes, stirring often. Remove from heat and cool.

Pour cooled orange juice mixture into aging container(s), add alcohol and water, stir to combine. Cap and let age at room temperature or cooler for 3 months.

After inital aging, strain liqueur mixture through a colander to remove the peel. (Discard peel or use in a recipe .) Re-strain through cloth until particles and sediment have been removed. Bottle and cap as desired. Continue aging for 3 more months.

*Variation: Substitute 2 cups 80-proof vodka or rum for the pure grain alcohol and 1 cup water if preferred.

**Microwave Directions: Substitute a large microwave-safe batter or mixing bowl for the saucepan. Microwave mixture on HIGH (100%) power for 4 to 5 minutes or until mixture comes to a boil; stir occasionally. After boil has been reached, reset to MEDIUM (50%) power and microwave for 8 to 10 minutes longer; stir every 2 minutes. Cool and continue as directed.

ORANGE CURAÇAO LIQUEUR

This liqueur is named after the Caribbean island of Curaçao where Spanish citrus groves were first planted. Bitter or sweet oranges may be used to make our natural liqueur. **Curaçao** *may also be tinted blue, green or a dark orange with food colors, to resemble commercial brands. Makes 1 fifth.*

4 large oranges
1 tsp. whole coriander seeds
1 cup pure grain alcohol and
1 cup water
2 Tbsp. orange juice (from oranges above)
2/3 cup granulated sugar
2/3 cup water

Place cake rack on cookie sheet. Turn oven to warm or lowest temperature.

Thinly peel the zest from oranges, using a swivel-bladed peeler or orange zester. Place peel on cake rack. Put in oven and leave until dry, about 1 hour. Let cool before continuing with recipe.

Crush coriander seeds coarsely with a pestle or back of a spoon in a mortar or bowl. Place seeds in aging container. Add dried zest, pure grain alcohol and the 1 cup water to the seeds. Squeeze fresh oranges and measure 2 tablespoons juice. Add to the aging container. Stir to combine. Cap and let age for 1 1/2 to 2 weeks, shaking once or twice.

After initial aging prepare sugar syrup. Combine sugar and 2/3 cup water in small saucepan. Bring to a boil, turn heat down and stir continuously until all sugar is dissolved. Remove from heat and let cool.

Strain orange mixture by pouring through cloth bag placed in a strainer over a large bowl. Rinse out aging container. Pour strained liqueur back into aging container. Add cooled syrup to liqueur. Cap and let age in a cool dark place for 3 to 4 months.

PEACH LIQUEUR

Our version of Southern Comfort

Use fresh peaches, any variety. Save the peaches after straining and serve over ice cream. Top a peach pie with whipped cream and liqueured peaches - wow! Ready in just over 1 month. Makes about 1 fifth.

1 1/2 lbs. peaches
1 cup granulated sugar
4 strips lemon peel
2 cups bourbon **or** brandy*

Peel, pit, and slice peaches. Place in saucepan.** Add sugar, stir well to combine. Warm over low heat until sugar is well dissolved and peaches are juicy. Place peach mixture into aging container. Add lemon peels and bourbon, stirring to combine. Cover container and put in a cool, dark place, or refrigerate if necessary. Let stand for 1 week, stirring occasionally.

After 1 week aging, strain liqueur mixture through medium wire strainer placed over a large mixing bowl. Press out liqueur liquid in peaches by pressing with the back of a wooden spoon. Either discard peach pulp or save for use in other recipes. Restrain through finer wire-mesh or cloth until desired clarity is reached. Bottle as desired. Liqueur is fine for cooking at this point and is drinkable. Improves with additional aging.

Variations: Spiced Peach Liqueur may be made by adding 2 cinnamon sticks and 4 whole cloves to this recipe.

*A Vodka-based liqueur may be made by substituting an 80-proof Vodka for either the bourbon or the brandy in this Peach Liqueur. The result will be a very natural, fruity liqueur.

Microwave Directions: Place peaches and sugar into large microwave safe mixing bowl. Stir to combine. Microwave on **HIGH (100%) power for 6 to 7 minutes, stirring every 2 minutes. Proceed as directed.

PIÑA COLADA LIQUEUR

*The Piña Colada cocktail has made this liqueur famous. Made with white Caribbean rum aged in oak casks, **Piña Colada Liqueur** will bring back memories of white beaches, crystal waters and tropical sea breezes at a moment's notice. Ready in 2 to 3 months. Makes approximately 1 quart.*

1 1/2 cups granulated sugar
1 1/2 cups water
2 cups packaged flaked coconut
1 vanilla bean, split
24 chunks (approximately 1 1/4 cups) fresh-cooked **or**
     canned unsweetened pineapple, drained
3 cups light rum

Bring water and sugar to a boil. Reduce heat to low; add coconut and vanilla bean. Simmer 5 minutes, uncovered, stirring frequently. Remove from heat; add pineapple. Cool to lukewarm. Add rum. Place in aging container and let stand for 1 month, shaking once a week.

Pour through a fine wire-mesh strainer into a large bowl. Press coconut and pineapple with potato masher or the back of a wooden spoon to obtain all the juice. Remove fruit. Strain liqueur through fine cloth or paper coffee filters several times until desired clarity is reached. Bottle and age an additional 1 to 2 months. If there is sediment at the bottom of the bottle, a final straining or siphoning may be needed at this time. If you prefer, the bottom cloudy layer may be saved for cooking.

PLUM LIQUEUR

Use any type of fresh plums in this recipe; each type gives its own distinctive flavor. Ready in 2 months. Makes about 1 quart.

2 lbs. plums
2 cups granulated sugar
2 cups vodka
1/2 cup brandy

Wash plums and pat dry. Cut plums in halves or smaller; pit. Place plums in aging container. Pour sugar over plums; stir. Add vodka and brandy, stirring to partly dissolve sugar. Cap container and place in a cool, dark place for 2 months; stir occasionally.

Place strainer over large bowl and strain liqueur. Press liquid from plums with the back of a wooden spoon. Discard plum pulp. Re-strain liqueur through cloth until clear. Bottle as desired. Ready for cooking or drinking but best if aged another month.

JAPANESE PLUM LIQUEUR

This plum liqueur is so outstanding in aroma, taste and color that it consistently is voted Number One in our liqueur classes. Japanese Plums are very small plums on the distinctive deep purple-leaf trees so common in many parts of the country. Because its pits are so large, many leave the fruits for the birds to enjoy. This recipe, however, requires no pitting and is very easy to make! Ready in 3 months. Makes over 1 quart.

2 lbs. Japanese plums
2 1/4 cups granulated sugar
2 3/4 cups vodka
1 cup brandy

Wash plums and pat dry. Cut each plum with knife to open but do not pit. Place plums into a large aging container. Add sugar, vodka and brandy to plums, stirring to combine. Cover or cap container and let age in a cool, dark place for 3 months; stir monthly.

After initial aging, strain liqueur mixture through wire mesh strainer placed over large mixing bowl. Press out liqueur in plums with back of a wooden spoon. Discard plums. Re-strain through cloth until clear. Bottle as desired. Liqueur is ready to serve but as with most liqueurs, it improves with additional aging.

37

POMEGRANATE LIQUEUR

A delicate liqueur with a jewel-like color and a gourmet taste. Truly outstanding. Ready in 2 months. Makes about 1 fifth.

2 large ripe pomegranates
1 to 1 1/2 cups granulated sugar, to taste
3/4 cup water
2 cups vodka **or** light rum
1 Tbsp. glycerine

Cut pomegranates in quarters. Pull back and remove one membrane at a time, exposing clusters of juicy red seeds. Gently pull seeds away from white centers. Place all seeds in aging container. Discard white membrances, centers and peels. Crush seeds slightly with back of a large wooden spoon.

Heat water and sugar together, stirring frequently, until well dissolved. Let cool. Pour vodka and sugar-water over seeds. Stir and let cool. Cap and place in a cool, dark place. Let age 1 month.

After initial aging, strain through a fine wire-mesh strainer. Discard seeds. Clean out aging container. Place strained liqueur into container. Add glycerine. Age at least 1 more month. Re-strain through cloth, until clear. Re-bottle as desired

---

QUICK PARFAIT AMOUR

This classic violet-colored French liqueur was once used as a love potion. Ready in just 2 weeks. Makes about 1 quart.

1 1/2 tsp. lemon extract
1/4 tsp. orange extract
1 3-inch piece vanilla bean **or** 1/4 tsp. vanilla extract
4 to 6 flower petals, rose, pansy **or** violet (optional)
3 1/2 cups vodka
1/2 cup brandy
1 1/2 cups granulated sugar
3/4 cup water

1 tsp. glycerine
3 drops red food coloring (optional)
1 drop blue food coloring (optional)

Combine extracts, vanilla bean, flower petals, vodka and brandy in a 1 1/2 quart or larger aging container. Cap and let age for 2 weeks in a cool, dark place. Strain liqueur through a wire-mesh strainer. Clean out aging container. Return liqueur to container.

In a saucepan combine sugar and water. Bring to a boil, then turn heat down, stirring constantly until sugar is dissolved. Set aside to cool. When cool, add sugar-water to liqueur, stirring to combine. Add glycerine and food coloring if desired. Let stand 24 hours before serving.

RHUBARB LIQUEUR

Don't pass this one by! It is delicately colored and captures the fresh rhubarb essence. Add some of this rosy liqueur to your next rhubarb pie. Wow! Ready in 2 months. Makes about 1 quart.

4 cups fresh rhubarb
3 cups granulated sugar
3 cups vodka

Wash and trim rhubarb. Slice rhubarb about 1/4" thick by hand or in the food processor. Place rhubarb in aging container. Add sugar and stir. Pour vodka over mixture and stir again. Cap or cover and let sit at room temperature for 2 to 4 weeks. The color will change to a rosy glow. Stir occasionally.

After initial aging, strain liqueur through metal colander placed over a large bowl. Press juice out of rhubarb with spoon. Discard rhubarb. Strain again through cloth until clear. Re-bottle as desired, cap and age at least 1 additional month before serving.

RASPBERRY LIQUEUR

Our version of Liqueur de Framboise

A favorite for its magnificent color and taste! Make it once and you'll make it again. This recipe also works well with most all cane berries, such as Blackberries, Loganberries, Marion-berries, etc. Ready in 3 months. Makes over 1 quart.

1 lb. fresh raspberries*
1 lb. granulated sugar
2 cups water
2 cups pure grain alcohol**, mixed with
2 cups water

Rinse and check raspberries, discard any overripe or moldy berries. Place raspberries into large bowl. Crush berries slightly with back of wooden spoon. Set aside.

Warm pint of water with sugar in medium saucepan over moderate heat. Stir continuously until well dissolved and liquid is warm. Pour sugar-water over raspberries, stir. Cover with plastic wrap and refrigerate for one week. Stir occasionally.

After refrigerator aging, strain mixture through fine wire mesh strainer into a large bowl or aging container. Add alcohol mixture, stir. Cap and let age 1 month.

Strain through cloth until clear. Re-bottle as desired. Ready for use in cooking at this point but age 2 months or longer before drinking.

*Note: Berry Liqueur - Use this same recipe for all types of cane berries such as Blackberry, Boysenberry, Loganberry, Marionberry, etc.

**Variation: 4 cups 80-proof vodka may be substituted for the 2 cups pure grain alcohol and 2 cups water. Proof of liqueur will be slightly less.

SPICED BERRY BRANDY

A wonderfully rich brandy-based liqueur that can be made with a variety of cane berries. Our favorites are Blackberries, wild or cultivated, Marionberries or plump Boysenberries. A sip of this in the winter is summer remembered. Makes an especially lovely gift. Ready in 1 month. Makes about 3 quarts.

4 qts. berries
1 qt. water
granulated sugar*
spices of choice:
1/2 tsp. whole cloves
1/2 tsp. whole allspice
2 cinnamon sticks
1 whole nutmeg
1 qt. unflavored brandy

Rinse and check berries in cool, tap water. Discard any overripe or moldy berries. Put berries and water into large enamel pot or kettle. Stir occasionally while mixture comes to a boil. After mixture has reached a boil, reduce heat just enough to maintain a low boil. Cook for 12 to 15 minutes or until berries lose shape, stirring every few minutes. Strain mixture, discarding berry pulp. Measure strained berry liquid and set aside.

Clean out the pot. Pour strained berry liquid back into pot. Add 1 1/2 to 2 cups sugar for each quart of berry liquid. Stir in sugar. Select some or all of spices and put in spice bag. Add to berry mixture. Heat mixture, stirring often, until mixture comes to a boil. Reduce heat until low boil is just maintained and time for 12 minutes. Remove spices and let cool slightly.

Add brandy to cooled mixture. Stir to combine. Bottle as desired, cap and store in a cool, dark place for 4 weeks.

*Variation: Sweetness may be varied in this recipe. Use at least 1 1/2 cups sugar per quart of berry liquid and not more than 2 cups sugar per quart of berry liquid for best results.

STRAWBERRY LIQUEUR I

Our version of Liqueur de Fraises

Pick fresh cultivated or wild strawberries for this delicate liqueur. For the best flavor use only fresh berries and prepare while at their peak of freshness. Ready in 31/2 months. Makes about 1 fifth.

3 cups fresh strawberries
1/2 cup powdered sugar
2 cups vodka
1/2 cup granulated sugar
2 Tbsp. water

Wash and stem berries. Pat dry. Halve berries and place in aging container. Cover berries with powdered sugar. Pour vodka over sugared berries. Stir just to combine. Cap container and let age in a cool, dark place for 2 to 3 weeks.

After initial aging period, combine granulated sugar and water in small saucepan.* Heat and stir until sugar is well dissolved. Set aside to cool.

Strain berry liquid through wire mesh strainer placed over large bowl. With the back of a wooden spoon crush out liqueur liquid caught in berries. Discard berry pulp. Re-strain mixture through cloth to further remove sediment. Add cooled sugar-water mixture to strained strawberry liqueur. Stir to combine. Re-bottle as desired. Age at least 1 month before serving.

***Microwave Directions:** Combine granulated sugar and water in a glass 1 cup measure, stir. Microwave on **HIGH (100%)** power for 30 seconds more. Stir to dissolve all sugar. Set aside to cool. Follow remaining directions.

STRAWBERRY LIQUEUR II

Another version of Liqueur de Fraises

A larger, but easy, recipe to catch the fleeting fresh strawberry season. Use sweet, ripe berries but be careful to avoid overripe and/or moldy berries. Ready in 2 months. Makes about 1 1/2 quarts.

1 fifth (750 ml) vodka
1 1/4 cups granulated sugar
4 cups sliced fresh strawberries

In large aging container, (or divide into two), combine sugar and vodka. Stir well to partly dissolve. Add strawberries, stir. Cap container. Stir or shake container daily for 2 weeks, or until sugar is completely dissolved.

When sugar is dissolved, place in cool, dark place for 6 weeks. Strain off strawberries after second aging. Discard berry pulp. Re-strain through fine muslin or coffee filters for clarity. Bottle as desired.

Variation: Wild Strawberry Liqueur is made with the same recipe. Wild strawberries are sometimes more tart and usually smaller. Sweetness may be increased if desired, but often the refreshing tartness of the wild strawberries is enjoyed by following the recipe exactly.

TABOO LIQUEUR

Our version of Forbidden Fruits

*This wonderful liqueur made from a mixture of fresh citrus fruits is reminiscent of the famous **Forbidden Fruits Liqueur**. Our taste-test panel said this was one of the most exquisite tasting liqueurs they had sampled. Ready in 1 month, but improves with additional time. Makes over 1 quart.*

thin peel from 1 orange, chopped
thin peel from 1 lemon, chopped
1 cup freshly squeezed grapefruit juice (about 2 grapefruits)
1 cup freshly squeezed orange juice (2 to 3 oranges)
1/4 cup freshly squeezed lemon juice (1 lemon)
2 1/4 cups granulated sugar
4" piece of vanilla bean, split
1 cup brandy
1 cup vodka

In a medium saucepan, combine grapefruit, orange and lemon juice, peels, sugar and vanilla bean. Bring to a boil. Reduce heat; simmer, stirring frequently for 10 to 12 minutes. Cool to lukewarm.

Pour cooled mixture into aging container; add brandy and vodka. Allow liqueur to age for 3 weeks, then strain several times using successively finer strainers, or fine cloth. For maximum clarity, let liqueur stand for several days between strainings. Pour liqueur into bottles and cap.

Variations: Honey may be substituted for all or part of the sugar. American whiskey may be substituted for the brandy.

MAKING NON-FRUIT LIQUEURS

ADVOCAAT LIQUEUR

Our version of Dutch Advocaat and Eggnog Liqueur

"Advocaat" is a Dutch word which means "a drink for lawyers". Mild, velvety and quickly made any time of year, but especially popular during the Holiday season due to its similarity to eggnog. Ready in 2 to 3 weeks. Makes about 1 1/2 quarts.

1 1/4 cups granulated sugar
3/4 tsp. vanilla
1/2 tsp. lemon extract
1 cup vodka
5 whole eggs
1 egg yolk
2/3 cup evaporated milk

Note: Directions given are for blender or food processor preparation. Can be made in a bowl if beaten well.

Put sugar into blender or food processor with steel knife, blend. Add remaining ingredients and combine for 30 seconds or until mixed well. Pour into container/bottles, cap and refrigerate.

Age for 1 to 2 weeks to mellow. Color will intensify as it ages, reaching a more traditional light shade of yellow.

Variation: Brandy Advocaat is a brandied variation made by substituting 1/4 to 1/2 cup French Brandy for that same amount of vodka in the Advocaat recipe.

Note: Please see precautions regarding uncooked eggs on page 55.

AMARETTO LIQUEUR

*Our liqueur will remind you of the famous,oldest and best known almond liqueur in the world today,"**Amaretto di Saronno**". That liqueur has been made in Italy since the fifteenth century. Ours is ready in just 1 to 2 months. Makes about 1 fifth.*

1/2 lb. almonds
2 dried apricot halves, chopped
2 cups brandy
1/2 cup pure grain alcohol and
1/2 cup water
1 Tbsp. orange rind
1 1/4 cups granulated sugar
1/2 cup water
2 tsp. almond extract
1 tsp. glycerine

Chop almonds and place in aging container. Add brandy, grain alcohol and 1/2 cup water. Include some of the bitter white part of the orange rind when peeling orange. Add orange rind and apricots to brandy mixture. Stir, cap and age for 1 to 2 months in a cool, dark place. Stir and test almond flavor after 1 month to determine if additional aging is desired.

After intial aging, strain clear liqueur liquid through colander or wire mesh strainer into bowl. Re-strain through cloth bag to remove fine particles. (Almonds and dried apricots may be saved for cooking.)

Combine sugar and 1/2 cup water in a small saucepan. Bring to a boil, stirring constantly. Reduce heat and simmer until all sugar is dissolved. Remove from heat and let cool.

Add cooled sugar-water, almond extract and glycerine to aged liqueur. Re-bottle as desired. Liqueur is ready to serve but will continue to improve with additional aging.

ANGELICA LIQUEUR

A special liqueur that uses the herb Angelica, from friend and noted herb expert, Terry Tucker Francis. Angelica (Angelica archangelica) has a long history of use especially in Europe and the Scandinavian countries where it has been used in food, medicine and fragrance. Its essential oils lend flavoring to many liqueurs, including some famous ones, such as **Benedictine, Chartreuse, Ratifia d'Angelique** *and* **Vermouth.** *The dried angelica root is available from many health food and herb stores. Ready in 1 1/2 months. Makes about 1 pint.*

3 Tbsp. dried chopped angelica root
1 Tbsp. chopped almonds
1 allspice berry, cracked
1 one-inch piece of cinnamon stick, broken
3 to 6 anise **or** fennel seeds, crushed
1/8 tsp. powdered coriander seed
1 Tbsp. chopped fresh **or** 1 tsp. dried marjoram leaves
1 1/2 cups vodka
1/2 cup granulated sugar
1/4 cup water
1 drop each yellow and green food coloring (optional)

Combine all herbs, nuts and spices with vodka in 1-quart or larger aging container. Cap tightly and shake daily for 2 weeks. Strain through fine muslin cloth or coffee filter paper; discarding solids. Clean out aging container. Place strained liqueur liquid into clean aging container.

Place sugar and water in saucepan and stir to combine over medium heat.* When sugar is completely dissolved, set aside and let cool. When cool, combine with food coloring and add to liqueur liquid. Cap and allow to age and mellow in a cool, dark place for 1 month.

*Microwave Directions: This step may be done in the microwave oven using a glass bowl. Microwave on **HIGH (100%)** for 1 to 1 1/2 minutes, stirring every 30 seconds.

ANISETTE LIQUEUR

*Italian **Anisette** is an anise-flavored liqueur that is sweeter and gentler than the Greek **Ouzo**. Delightful in our buttery **Italian Anise Star Cookies**. Ready in 3 months. Makes about 1 quart.*

1 tsp. coriander seeds
5 tsp. anise extract
1 fifth vodka
2 cups light corn syrup

Crush coriander seeds in a mortar or small bowl, using pestle or back of spoon. Place in aging container and add other ingredients. Cap and shake well to combine. Let stand in a cool, dark place for 1 month, shaking every few days.

After initial aging, strain liqueur through a fine cloth bag placed in wire-mesh strainer, over a large bowl. Bottle and age an additional 2 months.

CARAWAY LIQUEUR

*Similar to **Kümmel** but slightly sweeter, made in the Scandinavian tradition. Ready in 1 to 1 1/2 months. Makes about 1 quart.*

2 Tbsp. caraway seeds, crushed
1 Tbsp. fennel seeds, crushed
1 tsp. coriander seeds
3 cups vodka
3/4 cup distilled water
1 1/2 to 2 cups granulated sugar

Combine spices with alcohol in a 1-quart or larger aging container. Cover and let stand for 7 to 14 days in a cool place. After initial aging, add sugar and water by the following method. Bring water to a boil and pour over sugar. Stir to dissolve completely and let cool. Strain off seeds by pouring through a mesh strainer. Re-strain through a finer strainer as necessary to remove all seed material. Then combine cool sugar mixture and liqueur into a clean aging container. Age in a cool, dark place for 3 to 4 weeks. Bottle as desired.

*Variation: Your choice of spices may be used in this liqueur. Caraway seeds are the base ingredient, but add fennel seeds, coriander seeds, juniper berries or other herbs, spices or seeds to your taste. Follow the general proportions in Caraway Liqueur recipe.

CHRISTMAS SPICED BRANDY

A holiday recipe from herbalist, Terry Tucker Francis. A wonderful gift for the holidays but you'll want to serve it year-round. Ready in 1 1/2 months. Makes about 1 fifth.

3 Tbsp. mixed spices (any combination of: broken cinnamon
  sticks, cracked allspice, cloves, allspice berries, grated ginger
  root, **or** fresh nutmeg*)
2 juniper berries
colored peel only, of one-half a tangerine, minced
2 cups brandy
3/4 cup brown sugar
1/2 cup granulated sugar
1/2 cup water

Combine chosen spices, tangerine peel and juniper berries with brandy in a 1-quart or larger aging container. Cap and store in a cool, dark place, shaking container and tasting once weekly for up to 3 weeks (until flavor is at its peak). Strain off spices and peel by pouring through muslin cloth or coffee filter paper. Discard spices and peel. Clean out aging container. Re-strain until clear. Place strained liqueur in clean aging conatiner.

Combine sugars and water in a small saucepan. Heat over medium heat, stirring constantly to combine. When sugars are completely dissolved, remove from heat and let cool. Slowly add cooled sugar mixture to liqueur liquid, stir well. Age an additional 3 to 4 weeks to age and mellow.

*Tip: Use only 1 or 2 cloves or allspice berries and a single scraping of nutmeg. Too much of these potent spices could overwhelm subtler flavors.

50

CRÈME DE CACAO LIQUEUR

Chocolate has been a favorite since the days of the Aztecs. One of the more exotic uses for chocolate is as a liqueur. The French **Crème de Cacao Liqueur** *is perhaps the most famous.*

Our chocolate liqueur may be made with your choice of a liquid chocolate or dry powdered cocoa. Ready in 2 months. Makes slightly less than 1 fifth.

1 cup granulated sugar*
1/2 cup water
6 oz. unsweetened liquid chocolate **or** 1/2 cup dry cocoa*
2 cups vodka
1 tsp. vanilla extract
1/2 tsp. glycerine

Combine sugar and water in small saucepan and heat until mixture comes to a boil. Reduce heat and stir constantly until sugar is completely dissolved. Set aside and let cool.

In aging container combine chocolate, vodka and vanilla extract, stirring well to combine. Add cooled sugar syrup. Stir, cap and stir or shake container weekly for 1 month. Store in a cool, dark place.

After initial aging, let sit undisturbed for 1 week then carefully pour off clear liqueur, leaving chocolate sediment behind. Discard sediment. Strain liqueur by placing a cloth bag inside a strainer set over a large bowl. Repeat as necessary for clarity. Add glycerine to strained liqueur. Bottle as desired and let age for an additional month.

*****Tips:** Use a high quality unsweetened cocoa for best results. A combination of brown and granulated sugars may be used.

CRÈME DE MENTHE LIQUEUR

*This more traditional **Crème de Menthe Liqueur** uses extract rather than fresh mint as in the **Fresh Mint Liqueur**. It can be made in the three commercial shades of clear, gold and green. Ready in 1 month. Makes approximately 1 1/4 quarts.*

4 cups granulated sugar
2 cups water
3 cups vodka
1 Tbsp. mint **or** peppermint extract
1 tsp. glycerine

In saucepan, combine sugar and water. Bring to a boil, stirring constantly. When sugar is dissolved, set aside to cool. In aging container, combine remaining ingredients. Add cooled sugar syrup, stirring to combine. Re-bottle now or after initial 1 month aging.

Variations: Gold Crème de Menthe is made by adding yellow food coloring, a touch of red, and the merest hint of blue, by drops, to the basic clear recipe until desired color is achieved. (We suggest that you practice with food coloring and water first!) Age as directed.

Green Crème de Menthe: Add green and blue food coloring, by drops, until desired color is reached. Age as directed.

DUTCH CHOCOLATE-MINT LIQUEUR
Our version of Vandermint

A perfect liqueur to serve in place of dessert. Ready in 1 day. Makes about 1/2 pint.

1 cup **Crème de Cacao Liqueur**, fully aged
1/4 tsp. mint extract (spearmint, peppermint, **or** both)
1 Tbsp. brandy

Combine all ingredients in aging container. Cap and let stand 24 hours. Re-bottle if desire. Serve.

FRESH MINT LIQUEUR

*In our search for natural-based liqueurs, we automatically turned to our home-grown mint beds to reproduce **Crème de Menthe Liqueur**. What we achieved was a fresher, milder, more delicate liqueur that is in many ways superior to the classic. You may wish to try both recipes to discover your own preference. Ready in 1 1/2 to 3 months. Makes approximately 1 quart.*

1 1/4 cups fresh mint leaves, slightly packed
3 cups vodka
2 cups granulated sugar
1 cup water
1 tsp. glycerine
8 drops green food coloring
2 drops blue food coloring

Wash leaves in cold water several times. Shake or pat dry gently. Snip each leaf in half or thirds; discard stems. Measure cut mint leaves, packing slightly.

Combine mint leaves and vodka in aging container. Cap and let stand in a cool place for 2 weeks, shaking occasionally.

After initial aging, pour liqueur through colander into a large bowl to remove leaves; discard leaves.

In saucepan, combine sugar and water. Bring to a boil, stirring constantly. Let cool. Add cooled sugar syrup to mint liqueur base, stirring to combine. Add glycerine and food color; pour into aging container for secondary aging of 1 to 3 more months.

Variation: Fresh Crème de Menthe - If you like a slightly heavier emphasis on the mint, adjust to taste by adding drops of mint extract (up to 1 teaspoon) to Fresh Mint Liqueur.

AQUAVIT

A Scandinavian drink that is traditionally served ice-cold in small glasses. Serve with cheeses, seafood or smorgasbord. Often chased with a golden beer. Best made with a high quality vodka. Ready in 3 weeks. Makes 1 fifth.

1 Tbsp. caraway seeds*
1 fifth vodka

Bruise seeds by crushing with pestle or back of spoon in mortar or bowl. Add to vodka. Cap and let stand in cool, dark place for 3 weeks. Strain off seeds. Re-strain for clarity.

*Variation: Additional spices such as cardamon or anise may be added as desired.

GRAND ORANGE-COGNAC LIQUEUR
Our version of Grand Marnier

Make with good cognac or French brandy. Ready in 5 months. Makes about 1 pint.

1/3 cup orange zest*
1/2 cup granulated sugar
2 cups cognac **or** French brandy
1/2 tsp. glycerine

Place zest and sugar in a small bowl. Mash together with the back of a wooden spoon or pestle. Continue until sugar is absorbed into zest. Place in aging container. Add cognac. Stir, cap and age in a cool, dark place 2 to 3 months, shake monthly.

After initial aging, pour through fine mesh strainer placed over medium bowl. Rinse out aging container. Pour glycerine into aging container and place cloth bag inside strainer. Pour liqueur back through cloth bag. Stir with a wooden spoon to combine. Cap and age 3 more months before serving.

*Note: Seville oranges produce the authentic taste but any type of orange peel/zest may be used with good results.

54

H & C's IRISH CREAM LIQUEUR

*In our testing for an **Irish Cream Liqueur**, we used, as our standard, **Bailey's Original Irish Cream** - so good and so expensive! We found this one of the most difficult liqueurs to reproduce. We tried lots of 'homemade' recipes, but all missed the mark of our standard: the best. So we threw everything out (except the Bailey's) and started again. Relax; we finally got it— great, inexpensive, quick and easy! Ready in just 1 week. Makes approximately 1 fifth. Serve within 6 months.*

2 eggs
1 1/3 cups evaporated milk
1/2 tsp. chocolate syrup
1 Tbsp. pure vanilla extract
1/3 tsp. lemon extract
1/4 tsp. instant coffee
3/4 cup granulated sugar
1 3/4 cups Irish whiskey

Place all ingredients in blender; blend well. Bottle and let mellow in refrigerator at least one week before serving. We found this best after 1 to 2 weeks. Store in refrigerator.

Note: Due to the problem in some parts of the country where some eggs have been found containing the bacteria salmonella, we would suggest basic precautions when preparing food or drink containing uncooked eggs. Always start with clean, uncracked eggs. Refrigerate liqueur. Avoid serving to high risk persons—children, elderly and pregnant.

We are not aware, as of this print date, of any studies that have been made using raw eggs in an alcohol mixture. We would welcome any new information on such studies.

ITALIAN GOLD LIQUEUR

Our version of Galliano

Liquore Galliano, that brilliant yellow liqueur in the tall, skinny bottle, is a popular challenge to the "at-home" liqueur maker and is one of the most difficult to copy precisely. We tested countless recipes that didn't come close to the original, before developing a quality liqueur of sufficient complexity that did.

Almost without exception, every homemade recipe we found used 80 proof vodka. However, in our search for authentic flavor, we found that a stronger base was mandatory. Therefore, we used pure grain alcohol and suggest that you follow our guidelines. 100 proof vodka, where available, would be an adequate substitute. Ready in 3 to 6 months. Makes approximately 1 quart.

1 tsp. chopped, dried angelica root
1 3" cinnamon stick
1 whole clove
1 pinch nutmeg
1 vanilla bean, split
2 1/2 cups water*
2 cups granulated sugar
1 Tbsp. lemon juice
1/2 tsp. anise extract
1/2 tsp. banana extract
1/2 tsp. (scant) pineapple extract
1 1/2 cups pure grain alcohol*
1 tsp. glycerine
2 to 3 drops yellow food coloring

Line a wire-mesh strainer with a paper coffee filter. Set strainer over a one-quart mixing bowl.

Place dried angelica root, cinnamon, clove, nutmeg and vanilla bean in a medium saucepan. Add water; heat until mixture comes to a boil. Remove from heat. Let stand 15 seconds, then pour through the prepared strainer into the bowl. (It is important to work quickly or spices will impart too strong a color and taste to the liquid.) Reserve the vanilla; discard the other spices.

Rinse the saucepan and pour the liquid back into it. Add the reserved vanilla bean and the sugar. Heat until mixture comes to a boil; reduce heat and simmer 1 minute, stirring constantly. Remove from heat and cool to room temperature.

When cool, add the lemon juice, extracts, and alcohol, stirring to combine. Pour into aging container. Cap and let age in a cool, dark place for 1 week.

After initial aging, strain through a cloth bag set in a wire-mesh strainer over a large bowl. Repeat until desired clarity is reached. Stir in glycerine and food coloring. Bottle, seal and age for 3 to 6 months.

*Note: If substituting 100 proof vodka for the alcohol, use 3 cups of vodka and reduce the water to 1 cup.

ITALIAN HAZELNUT LIQUEUR

Our version of Frangelico

*Oregon hazelnuts are a key ingredient in this simulation of the delicate Italian **Frangelico Liqueur**. Ready in 6 months. Makes about 1 quart.*

4 cups (about 1 1/8 lb.) unshelled hazelnuts (filberts)
1 tsp. chopped dried angelica root
1/2 vanilla bean, split
1 fifth vodka
1/4 tsp. almond extract
1 1/2 cups granulated sugar
1 cup water
1 tsp. glycerine
1 to 2 drops yellow food coloring (optional, to correct color if necessary)

Preheat oven to 350° F. Shell hazelnuts. Coarsely chop hazelnuts and place them on a baking sheet in the oven for 10 to 15 minutes. Remove from oven and place in an aging container. Stir in dried angelica root, vanilla bean, vodka and almond extract. Cap and let age for 1 month in a cool, dark place, shaking occasionally.

After aging, pour through fine mesh strainer into a large bowl. Rinse out aging container. Place cloth bag or triple cheesecloth inside large funnel. Place funnel over aging container and pour liqueur through.

In medium saucepan, combine sugar and water; bring to a boil. Immediately reduce heat and simmer for a few minutes, stirring to dissove sugar completely. Let cool. When sugar syrup has cooled, add to aging container, stirring well to combine. Cap and let age 3 months.

After second aging, re-strain through cloth or paper coffee filters until desired clarity is reached. Stir in glycerine and food coloring, if desired. Let age 2 more months before serving.

ITALIAN HERB LIQUEUR

Our version of Strega

The noted Italian herbal liqueur, **Strega***, is made with over 70 herbs. It was also used as a love potion in days gone by. We hope you'll love our simplified recipe. Ready in 2 months. Makes about 1 quart.*

6 cardamom pods
1 Tbsp. star anise **or** anise seed
1 Tbsp. chopped, dried angelica root
1 3" cinnamon stick
2 cloves
1/4 tsp. mace
1 fifth vodka
1 cup honey

In small mortar, crush cardamom seeds (which have been removed from pods). Add star anise and break up slightly. Place into 1 1/2-quart or larger aging container. Add remainder of herbs. Stir in vodka. Cap and let age in a cool, dark place for 1 week.

After initial aging, strain off all seeds through metal strainer. Re-strain through coffee filter or muslin cloth bag to remove tiny particles. Wash and dry aging container. Pour clear herbal liquid back into aging container. Stir in the 1 cup of honey. Cap and age in a cool, dark place for 8 weeks. Do not move or stir this liqueur during second aging, this will allow the cloudiness from the honey to settle. Siphon off the clear liqueur. See siphoning directions on page 14. Bottle as desired.

KÜMMEL LIQUEUR

*Caraway seeds, which are actually the dried fruit of the Carum Carvi plant, are the predominant flavoring in this Old World liqueur. The versatile **Kümmel** will become a favorite before-dinner apéritif or an after-dinner refresher, as well as an unique ingredient in many drinks. Used in cooking, it will lace your breads, vegetables, sausages and pork dishes with its warm, aromatic goodness. Ready in 1 1/2 to 2 months. Makes just over 1 fifth.*

2 1/2 Tbsp. caraway seeds
1/4 tsp. fennel seeds
2 whole cloves
3 cups vodka **or**
1 1/2 cups pure grain alcohol **and**
1 1/2 cups water
1/2 cup water
2/3 cup granulated sugar

'Bruise' caraway and fennel seeds with pestle or the back of a wooden spoon. Place in aging container with whole cloves. Stir in vodka or pure grain alcohol and 1 1/2 cups water. Cap and let stand 24 hours. Remove cloves, recap and let age 2 to 3 more weeks in a cool, dark place. Shake occasionally.

After initial aging, strain off seeds. Combine sugar and water in a saucepan and heat to a boil, stirring to dissolve sugar. Remove from heat and let cool. Add cooled sugar syrup to liqueur; stir. Cap and age 1 to 2 months more.

Re-strain, if necessary, to make liqueur particle-free. Re-bottle as desired.

MEXICAN COFFEE LIQUEUR

Our version of Kahlúa

*No book on liqueur making would be complete without a coffee liqueur recipe similar to **Kahlúa**. Research was no problem, since almost everyone gave us their 'Kahlúa' recipe. We hoped one of them would be perfect, so we could move on to the other liqueurs. However, this turned out to be one of the more difficult liqueurs to simulate accurately. There were glaring errors in the majority of the 'homemade' liqueurs (and some of these are even in print!) **Kahlúa** is actually a complex liqueur. We do not recommend using brown sugar or just vodka. Try this recipe and we think you will agree it is an accurate resemblance of classic **Kahlúa**. Ready in 2 to 4 months. Makes about 1 1/2 quarts.*

2 cups water
1/4 cup plus 2 tsp. instant coffee granules **or** powder*
3 1/2 cups granulated sugar
1 vanilla bean, split
2 3/4 cups vodka
3/4 cup brandy
1/4 tsp. chocolate extract
1 drop red food coloring

Heat water in medium saucepan. When hot, add coffee and stir until dissolved. Add sugar and vanilla bean, stirring well to combine. Bring to a boil, stirring constantly. Immediately reduce heat so that a very low boil is maintained for 1 minute. Remove from heat and cool to lukewarm.

Pour vodka and brandy into aging container. Add the cooled coffee mixture and the chocolate extract. Stir well. Cap and let age in a cool, dark place for 3 weeks.

After initial aging, strain liqueur through a cloth-lined wire-mesh strainer over a large bowl. Repeat until desired clarity is reached. Stir in food coloring. Bottle, cap and let age an additional 1 to 3 months.

*Note: For best results use a freshly opened jar of coffee.

OLD JAMAICA COFFEE LIQUEUR

Our version of Tia Maria

*There are many well-known coffee liqueurs, but one of the most popular is the Jamaican **Tia Maria**. Our rum-based recipe is similar to this famous liqueur.*

Naturally, the taste will vary depending upon the types of rum and coffee used. For authenticity, use Jamaican light rum and a premium quality instant coffee. Ready in 2 to 3 months. Makes approximately 1 1/2 quarts.

2 1/2 cups water
1/4 cup instant coffee granules **or** powder*
2 cups granulated sugar
1 vanilla bean, split
1 fifth light rum
1 1/2 tsp. glycerine, optional

Heat water in a medium saucepan. When hot, stir in coffee until dissolved. Add sugar and vanilla bean, stirring to combine. Bring to a boil, lower heat and simmer for one minute, stirring constantly. Remove from heat; cool to lukewarm.

When cool, add rum; stir well. Pour into aging container; cover tightly and allow the liqueur to age 3 weeks in a cool, dark place.

After initial aging, strain liqueur through a cloth-lined wire-mesh strainer over a large bowl. Add glycerine, re-bottle, and age an additional 1 to 3 months.

***Note:** A freshly opened jar of coffee will give best results.

NASSAU VANILLA LIQUEUR

Our version of Nassau Royale

*This dark rum-based liqueur is similar to the well-known **Nassau Royale**. It may be served at room temperature or slightly warm, in the tradition of **Amaretto Liqueur** or a fine brandy. Ready in 2 to 3 months. Our recipe makes just under a quart.*

2 1/2 cups dark rum
4 vanilla beans*, split in half
1 cup granulated sugar
1 cup water
1 tsp. glycerine

Combine rum and vanilla beans in aging container. Cap and shake to mix. Age in a cool, dark place for 2 to 3 weeks.

In a small saucepan combine sugar and water. Stir over medium heat until mixture comes to a boil. Remove from heat; continue stirring until all sugar is dissolved. Let cool.

Strain liqueur by pouring through coffee filter or cloth bag placed in strainer over medium bowl. Save vanilla beans.*

Combine cooled sugar syrup with liqueur. Stir in glycerine. Bottle, cap and age an additional 1 to 2 months before serving.

Microwave Directions: Combine sugar and water in a 2-cup glass measure. Microwave on **HIGH (100%)** power for 30 seconds. Stir with wooden spoon. Microwave for 30 to 45 seconds more. Remove from microwave and stir until all sugar is dissolved. Let cool and proceed as directed.

*Tip: See page 107 for **Vanilla Sugar** recipe. This is a great way to recycle vanilla beans used in liqueur making.

OUZO LIQUEUR

*You need the strength of a Greek god to drink **Ouzo**. This liqueur is an anise-flavored test of manhood that will delight some and flatten others. In cooking, use sparingly for its unique anise flavor. Ready in 3 months. Makes about 1 fifth.*

1/2 cup boiling water
4 tsp. granulated sugar
1/4 tsp. dried angelica root, chopped
  pinch of mace
4 tsp. anise extract
1 1/2 cups pure grain alcohol
3/4 to 1 cup water*

Combine boiling water and sugar in the aging container; stir or shake until sugar is dissolved. Stir in dried angelica root and mace. Cool to lukewarm, then add anise extract, pure grain alcohol and water. Shake to combine.

Cover and let stand for 3 days. Strain and re-bottle. Allow this liqueur to age for 1 month.

*Note: You may adjust the alcohol strength to your taste by adjusting the quantity of water as shown and still have an authentic Ouzo.

PIÑA COLADA LIQUEUR

See **Making Fruit Liqueurs Chapter,** page 36.

SCOTTISH HIGHLAND LIQUEUR

Our version of Drambuie

*The well-known and well-loved **Drambuie** is a Scottish tradition. As the legend is told, this herbal liqueur was once a favorite of Bonnie Prince Charlie, who in 1746 gave his secret recipe to the Mackinnons of Strathaird in gratitude for their shelter and assistance after his army was defeated.*

*The name **Drambuie** is derived from the Gaelic words 'an dram huidbeach' which means 'the drink that satisfies.' That phrase applies as well to our Scottish Highland Liqueur. One sip and you're sure to hear the bagpipes! Ready in 6 1/2 months. Makes 1 quart.*

1 fifth Johnny Walker Black Label Scotch*
1 1/2 cups mild honey
2 tsp. dried, chopped angelica root
1/4 tsp. fennel seeds, crushed
2 2" strips lemon zest

Combine all ingredients in aging container. Cover tightly and shake gently several times during the first 24 hours. After 24 hours, remove the lemon zest. Cover again and let stand in a cool, dark place for 2 weeks, shaking gently every other day.

Strain through a wire sieve to remove the angelica root and fennel. Return to aging container, cover and let stand undisturbed in a cool, dark place for 6 months. Siphon or pour clear liqueur into a sterile bottle. The cloudy dregs may be saved for cooking.

***Note:** We are very fussy about the scotch in this recipe! For best results use the recommended brand.

SERVING AND MIXING LIQUEURS

SERVING & MIXING LIQUEURS

Most liqueurs are excellent mixed in cocktails or punches. We particularly like the fruit liqueurs in tropical drinks and punches. A good example of this type of beverage is in **Long Life Wedding Punch.** Serve this punch at any special occasion.

One type of liqueur that is generally served with appetizers is a caraway-based liqueur such as **Kümmel.** Some strong-flavored liqueurs such as **Ouzo** or **Aquavit** are also best served before a meal. Pair these liqueurs with appetizers of hot or cold cheeses as well as seafood for a perfect match.

Traditionally, liqueurs are served at room temperature in small, stemmed liqueur glasses. Some liqueurs, such as Amaretto, can be served lightly warmed in a brandy snifter (small portions, please!) Liqueurs are commonly served with after-dinner coffee but you will find many other special times and ways to serve them.

BEVERAGES
WITH LIQUEURS

AMERICAN WHISKEY PUNCH

Makes just over 1 gallon. An easy-to-make and refreshing punch.

1 fifth whiskey
3 oz. **Curaçao** or other **Orange Liqueur**
6 oz. **California Lemon Liqueur**
4 cups orange juice
1 qt. iced tea
1 lemon, sliced
1 lime, sliced
1 qt. club soda
 ice

Combine first 5 ingredients in punch bowl. Decorate with fruit.
Add soda and ice before serving.

BANANA DAIQUIRI

A classic! Serves 1.

 juice of 1 lime
1 tsp. sugar
1 inch slice of banana
1 oz. light rum
 dash of **Cherry Liqueur**
 shaved ice
1 maraschino cherry with stem

Blend all ingredients, except cherry, in a blender or food processor. Pour into a chilled stemmed glass. Top drink with a
stemmed cherry.

BITTER LEMON HIGHBALL

*Pour 1 1/2 ounces of your favorite sweet liqueur into a highball
glass. Add ice and fill with Bitter Lemon soda. Stir well.*

CHRISTMAS CRANBERRY PUNCH

A bright and festive punch that brings sparkle to the season. Easily made from supplies that can be kept on hand. Recipe makes about 3 quarts, increase as needed.

1 qt. cranberry juice, well chilled
1 qt. lemon-lime soda, well chilled
1 cup vodka
2 Tbsp. lime juice
1 cup **Cranberry Liqueur**
1/2 cup **Orange Liqueur**
1 fresh orange, sliced
  sugar, optional, sweeten to taste if desired

Combine all ingredients, except orange slices in a punch bowl. Add ice block or ring and fresh orange slices. Serve.

CHRISTMAS TOASTS

May you be poor in misfortune this Christmas
and rich in blessings
slow to make enemies
quick to make friends
and rich or poor, slow or quick,
as happy as the New Year is long.

    - Irish Toast

Here's to us all
God bless us every one!

      - Tiny Tim's Toast
      from Charles Dickens'
      A Christmas Carol

CARIBBEAN COOLER

Serves 1.

1 1/2 oz. rum (light or dark)
2 oz. (1/4 cup) fresh or frozen strawberries, icy but thawed
1 oz. **Banana Liqueur**
1 oz. sweet and sour drink mix
  crushed ice

Combine all ingredients in a blender or food processor. Blend until smooth. Pour into a tall chilled glass.

FORBIDDEN FRUITS COCKTAIL

An elegant and fruity drink perfect for a special evening of entertaining. A make-ahead recipe that's easy on the host and hostess. Serve in champagne glasses if possible. Serves 8 to 10.

Fruit Base:
1/3 cup orange juice, fresh preferred
2 cups white Rhine wine, well chilled
1/4 cup **Cherry Liqueur**
1/8 cup **Black Currant Liqueur**
1/8 cup lemon juice
1 cup pineapple cubes, fresh or packed in natural juice
1 cup strawberries, fresh preferred
1/2 cup apple, diced
1 orange, peeled, sectioned and cut into quarters

Combine all fruit base ingredients in a large container, stir. Cover and chill overnight or for 24 hours.

Champagne:
1 to 2 bottles champagne, well chilled

Fill each champagne glass almost half full with fruit base mixture. Fill rest of glass with chilled champagne. Stir gently. Spear 1 piece of fruit with a toothpick and serve immediately.

LIQUEUR FRAPPÉ

For a simple but elegant drink, fill a stemmed glass with crushed ice. Pour 1 1/2 ounces of your favorite liqueur over ice. Serve.

HARVEY WALLBANGER

1 oz. vodka
1/2 oz. **Italian Gold Liqueur**
 Orange juice

Pour vodka into tall glass filled with ice cubes. Fill glass 3/4 full with orange juice. Stir. Float or stir in Italian Gold Liqueur.

KIR

*Kir, a French apéritif, is traditionally made with a dry white wine and **Crème de Cassis**. We have found that a number of liqueurs, especially fruit liqueurs may be substituted for flavor variety. Try your favorites served in a champagne glass or flute with either a slice of fruit, fresh strawberry or a twist of lemon. Easy and lovely. Serves 2.*

6 oz. dry white wine of choice, chilled
1 oz. **Crème de Cassis or** fruit liqueur of choice

Combine, garnish and serve.

LIQUEURED HOT CHOCOLATE

*If you aren't a coffee lover, we suggest hot chocolate. The addition of a small shot of a liqueur such as **Irish Cream,** **Mexican Coffee, Cherry**, etc. can turn an old standard into a hot drink with real pizazz.*

LIQUEUR COFFEE

*After-dinner liqueur coffee is easy to make when you have a selection of liqueurs on hand. Coffee served in this manner provides an elegant finish to a meal and may often be substituted for dessert. If your liqueur dictates, you may wish to top your coffee with sweetened whipped cream or **Whipped Liqueur Cream**. This may be served in demitasse or coffee cups, mugs, footed coffee cups or glasses, depending upon the occasion.*

*While almost any liqueur works well with coffee, some of our favorites are: **Amaretto, Crème de Menthe, Dutch Chocolate-Mint, Crème de Cacao, Cherry, Irish Cream, Mexican Coffee, Old Jamaican Coffee, Orange Curaçao** and **Scottish Highland Liqueurs**. Recipe makes about 6 ounces, enough for 1 coffee cup or 2 demitasse cups.*

5 oz. hot, freshly-brewed coffee
1/2 jigger (3/4 oz.) liqueur of choice

Brew coffee to strength desired. Pour liqueur into coffee cup(s). Pour coffee over liqueur; stir to blend. Top with either sweetened whipped cream or Whipped Liqueur Cream (see page 107) if desired. Serve immediately.

LONG LIFE WEDDING PUNCH

This outstanding punch was created by Cheryl Long for her wedding reception when she married a man named "Long". But it fits everyone, since tradition now dictates a toast to "Long Life" for the bride and groom. It is a very special blending of fruit liqueurs, champagne, fresh fruits, soda and a bit of Caribbean rum. A superb punch for special occasions. Of special note is the "Make-Ahead" directions for the fruit base. Recipe makes about 2 gallons, enough for 1 large punch bowl. Increase as needed. Enjoy!

Fruit Base:
Combine in a large bowl, (to hold about 1 gallon):
1 1/2 qts. white grape juice
1 cup powdered sugar
1 cup lemon juice
1/4 cup maraschino cherry juice
1/2 cup grenadine
2 cups pineapple juice
  juice of 4 fresh oranges
  pineapple chunks, cut from 1 fresh pineapple

Stir to combine all ingredients. Refrigerate until needed, (use in 24 hours) or follow Make Ahead Directions.

Make Ahead Directions For Fruit Base:
Follow directions but do not refrigerate. Instead place base in freezing containers, (allow ample air space for expansion, at least 1" depending upon size of container). Freeze. Two days before needed, place in refrigerator to thaw.

Bubbly Completion:
Combine base with the following in a large punch bowl and serve:
1 qt. club soda, well chilled
2 cups rum, light **or** dark
1/2 cup **Orange Liqueur**
1/2 cup **Pomegranate or** any **Cherry Liqueur**
3 bottles champagne, well chilled
  Ice block or ring, (optional, but nice with fruit slices)

WEDDING TOASTS

Grow old with me!
The best is yet to be,
The last of life,
For which the first is made.

- Robert Browning

May we all live to be present
At their Golden Wedding.
May you grow old on one pillow.

- Armenian Toast

LONG ISLAND ICED "TEA"

This drink is served just like tea, in frosty pitchers and tall glasses with ice. Refreshing but potent, this cocktail actually contains no tea at all! Serves 4.

1/3 cup **Orange Curaçao** or **Grand Orange-Cognac Liqueur**
1/4 cup cranberry juice
1/4 cup light rum
1/4 cup tequila
1/2 cup vodka
 ice cubes

Combine all ingredients in a pitcher. Add ice cubes to fill the pitcher; stir mixture well. Serve in highball glasses.

MAI TAI

Serves 1.

1 oz. light rum
1/2 oz. **Curaçao**
1/4 oz. orgeat syrup
1/2 oz. orange juice
1/2 oz. lime juice

Combine all ingredients in a double old-fashioned glass with ice.
Squeeze some lime juice into the drink and drop the shell into
the glass. Garnish as desired with cherry, orange slice and
pineapple.

LIQUEUR MILKSHAKE

*This liqueur milkshake makes 1 serving. You may change the
flavor of your milkshake by using any of the following liqueurs:*
***California Lemon, Crème de Menthe, Crème de Cacao, Crème
de Prunelle, Cherry, Dutch Chocolate-Mint, English Damson
Plum, Hawaiian Fruit, Italian Gold, Mexican Coffee, Old
Jamaican Coffee, Orange Curaçao, Piña Colada,*** *or* ***Taboo.***

1/3 cup liqueur of choice
1/4 cup crushed ice
1 scoop vanilla ice cream

Combine liqueur and ice in blender; process until well blended.
Add ice cream and blend just until combine.

Serve immediately in a chilled goblet and garnish as desired with
fresh fruit, chocolate curls, maraschino cherry, etc.

PLUM SPARKLER

Serves 1.
5 oz. white wine, chilled (such as a Chablis)
1 oz. **Plum Liqueur**
1 1/2 oz. club soda
1 twist of lemon peel
ice cubes

Pour wine over ice cubes in a tall, chilled glass. Stir in Plum Liqueur and soda. Top with lemon twist and serve.

RAMOS FIZZ

Serves 1.
1 1/2 oz. gin **or** vodka
1 oz. **Orange Liqueur**
3 oz. half and half
juice of 1/2 lemon
1 egg white
1 Tbsp. powdered sugar
1/4 cup shaved ice.

Combine all ingredients in blender or food processor. Blend until smooth and frothy. Pour into tall chilled glass.

Optional: Sprinkle with a bit of ground nutmeg.

RHUBARB COOLER

Serves 1.
Rhubarb Liqueur
orange juice
club soda
shaved ice

Combine equal amounts of Rhubarb Liqueur and orange juice. Pour enough of this mixture into a tall chilled glass filled with shaved ice to fill the glass two-thirds full. Add enough club soda to fill glass.

SANGRIA

Mix this in a large pitcher in front of your guests for party flair.
Makes about 2 quarts.

1 1/2 cups cracked ice
1/2 cup **Curaçao or** other **Orange Liqueur**
1/2 cup **California Lemon Liqueur**
1 fifth red wine (Burgundy **or** red table wine preferred)
2 thinly sliced oranges
1 thinly sliced lemon
2 Tbsp. granulated sugar
1 to 2 cups club soda

Place ice in pitcher. Combine all ingredients. Stir and serve.

A TOAST OF FRIENDSHIP

May the hinges of friendship never rust,
    nor the wings of love lose a feather.

- Dean Ramsay

STRAWBERRY MARGARITA

Serves 1.

1 1/2 oz. tequila
3/4 oz. Strawberry Liqueur
6 to 8 fresh strawberries
  splash of sweet and sour mix
  shaved ice

Blend in a shaker, blender or food processor. Pour into stemmed glass. Serve.

SCANDINAVIAN SPICED COFFEE

*A nice change of pace. Makes 4 regular servings or if preferred ,
8 demitasse cup servings.*

4 cups rich, hot coffee
1 cinnamon stick
6 whole allspice
1/8 tsp. ground cardamom
1/4 cup granulated sugar
4 fresh orange peel strips
4 Tbsp. **Orange Liqueur**
   sweetened, whipped cream, optional

Combine first six ingredients in medium saucepan. Heat gently,
stirring to dissolve sugar. When heated through, turn off heat,
cover and let stand for 15 to 20 minutes. Reheat and strain. Pour
into 4 cups, put 1 tablespoon liqueur in each cup. Top with
whipped cream, if desired, and serve immediately.

A CONGRATULATORY TOAST

You have deserved high commendation,
Irue applause and love.

- As you Like It, Act I

LIQUEURS ON ICE

*A light cocktail or summer cooler may be made very simply with
a variety of liqueurs. Fill an old-fashioned glass with ice cubes.
Pour liqueur of your choice over and serve.*

APÉRITIFS AND DIGESTIFS

Many liqueurs, primarily herbal ones, are often referred to as "apéritifs" or "digestifs." One of the best known ones is **Anisette**. This liqueur has an anise or licorice flavor and a French name. Greek **Ouzo**, a stronger liqueur, also has an anise flavor.

European caraway liqueurs are often called **Kümmel,** as is our German version. **Aquavit** is similar, but this Scandinavian apéritif is not sweet.

Apéritifs are generally served before a meal, often with appetizers or in place of them. The term "digestifs" refers to the digestive nature of some liqueurs. When used in this manner the liqueur is usually served after a meal. Either way they may be served in small liqueur glasses, sometimes chilled or on the rocks.

AQUAVIT IN AN ICE BLOCK

Aquavit should always be served ice cold. Here is a spectacular way to do so. Serve with appetizers, especially cheese and seafood.

Find a large, tall can that the Aquavit bottle will comfortably fit in. Pour about one-half inch of water in the bottom of the can and freeze the water (without the bottle in it this time). This forms a base. When frozen, place the bottle in the can and fill the can up with water. Freeze with the bottle in it.

When ready to serve, run hot water on the outside of the can until the ice melts enough to release the ice block. Now wrap the block in an attractive cloth napkin and pour for your delighted guests.

SKOALING

The popular Scandinavian toast is said in one word, skal, or skol, or as it has been anglicized, skoal. Somewhat similiar to our "cheers" but a bit more dignified, it generally means "a toast to you or your health".

COOKING WITH LIQUEURS

COOKING WITH LIQUEURS

Making your own liqueurs is just half the fun. The other half lies in using your liqueurs to add a gourmet touch to your special dishes. Even everyday fare can undergo a transformation with the addition of a dash of liqueur. For example, baste your pork roast or pork chops with **Crème de Prunelle** before roasting or broiling and see what that little difference can do. When you are making gravy from the drippings, be sure to add a spoonful or two of **Crème de Prunelle** for flavor enhancement.

Baking opens up a whole realm of opportunities for using your homemade liqueurs. While most of the alcohol will evaporate if baked at higher temperatures, the essence of liqueur still adds flavor to the recipe. Many breads and muffins can be topped with a **Liqueur Glaze** (see page 93) which is not cooked and therefore keeps its full strength and flavor. Pie fillings offer the experimental cook a wide range of possibilities. One of our favorites is the addition of a couple of tablespoons of **Apple Liqueur** to apple, raisin or mince pie fillings. Extraordinarily good!

It is no accident that liqueurs are added to the recipes in this book. In developing them, we set high standards. Each recipe and liqueur is a marriage of flavors; one would not be complete without the other. Browse through the recipes and start with some of your favorites. We hope you'll try them all.

GOLDEN CREAM

*True **Galliano** lovers will be delighted with this recipe. It blends our **Italian Gold Liqueur** with fresh pineapple and creamed cheese for an unique topping or dip. Try it spooned over pound or tea cake, dip homemade doughnuts or beignets into it, or spread it on French toast, waffles or hot bran muffins. Makes about 2 1/2 cups.*

1/2 cup (1 stick) unsalted butter
8 oz. (1 large package) cream cheese
1 cup confectioners' sugar
2 Tbsp. **Italian Gold Liqueur**
3/4 cup fresh pineapple chunks*

Cut butter and cream cheese into chunks. Place in food processor work bowl fitted with steel knife. Add powdered sugar and process until mixture is creamed. Add liqueur and pulse to combine. Add pineapple chunks and process by pulsing off and on until pineapple is in small chunks and mixture is well combined.

Alternate method: If preferred, use a hand or electric mixer to make this recipe. Cut pineapple chunks smaller and stir into creamed mixture.

*Fresh pineapple is preferred but pineapple canned in natural juice may be substituted. Drain well before use.

FRENCH COUNTRY PÂTÉ

*An ideal recipe for entertaining. Easy when made in the food processor and best made ahead of time. The **Crème de Prunelle,** (a classic French prune liqueur), adds mellowness to this mildly flavored pâté. Makes about 2 cups. Serve with **Seasoned Melba Toast.***

2 medium onions
  cooking oil (canola, safflower, etc. preferred)
1 lb. fresh chicken livers, washed and patted dry
  flour
  seasoning salt and pepper, to taste
1 Tbsp. **Crème de Prunelle**
2 Tbsp. cut liqueured prunes, (optional but good)*

Peel onions and cut into fourths. Coarsely chop onions in a food processor with a steel knife. Place a thin layer of oil in a large frying pan. Add onions and sauté until medium brown in color. Remove onions from frying pan and set aside. Dip chicken livers into a mixture of flour, seasoning salt and pepper. Add additional oil to frying pan as necessary. Sauté chicken livers over medium-low heat until no pink remains.

Place cooked chicken livers, onions, Crème de Prunelle, prunes and any cooking oil left in pan (oil is optional), into the food processor work bowl. Process with steel knife until well blended, scraping down sides of bowl with spatula as necessary. Spoon into serving container. Pat flat on the top. Cover with plastic wrap and refrigerate 8 hours or overnight before serving.

*Prunes saved from making Crème de Prunelle.

SEASONED MELBA TOAST

*The perfect accompaniment to **French Country Pâtè**. Simple, but delicious and economical to make.*

1 long French bread or baguette
seasoning salt **or** seasoning non-salt may be substituted

Preheat oven to 350°F. With a sharp knife, slice bread into 1/4" thick slices. Lay slices on cookie sheets, spacing so sides do not touch. Lightly sprinkle all slices with seasoning salt. Bake for 20 minutes, or until lightly browned and dry to the touch. Remove from oven and let stand at room temperature until cool and crisp. Place in dry plastic bags. Seal and set aside until needed. May be made up to 1 week prior to use. Keeps well.

HEAVENLY CREAM CHEESE

We get so many raves over this very easy recipe, it's almost embarrassing! This can be used on almost anything. Excellent on nut breads, pound cake, cookies, crackers and simply wonderful used as a cake filling and/or frosting. Makes about 2 cups.

8 oz. (large package) cream cheese
1/2 cup confectioners' sugar
1/2 cup liqueur of choice
3/4 cup chopped dried fruit*

Let cream cheese soften. Place in medium mixing bowl. Add sugar and half of the liqueur. Whip with whisk or beater. Add remaining liqueur, whip again. Check consistency, should be spreadable, add a small amount of liqueur if too thick. Does thicken when refrigerated. Fold in chopped fruit. Use as desired. Store in refrigerator.

*Tip: A handy time-saver is to use the pre-chopped dried fruit assortments now available in markets.

LEMON LIQUEUR TEA LOAF

Use the aromatic liqueured lemon peels saved from making **Lemon Liqueur** *in this versatile tea-time favorite. Makes 1 loaf.*

1/2 cup (1 stick) butter **or** margarine
1 cup granulated sugar
2 eggs
1 1/4 cups sifted, all-purpose flour
1 tsp. baking powder
  dash of salt, optional
1/2 cup milk
1/2 cup finely chopped walnuts
2 Tbsp. finely chopped lemon peel
5 Tbsp. **Lemon Liqueur**

Soften butter. Cream sugar and butter together then beat in eggs. Combine baking powder and salt with sifted flour. Add milk to egg mixture. Stir in flour mixture a little at a time, stirring well to combine. Finally, add nuts, 3 tablespoons lemon liqueur and lemon peel; stir well.

Spray a 5" x 9" loaf pan with vegetable coating spray or grease as desired. Bake in preheated 350° F oven for 55 to 60 minutes. Test with toothpick for doneness. Let cool. Poke a number of holes in the top of the loaf with a toothpick and pour 1 to 2 tablespoons Lemon Liqueur over the top. Serve warm or cool.

WHIPPED LIQUEUR BUTTER

Another wonderful basic recipe you can have some fun with. Try a variety of flavors to find your favorites. Makes about 2/3 cup.

1/2 cup (1 stick) unsalted butter
1 Tbsp. honey
1/4 tsp. grated fresh lemon peel
1/4 cup liqueur of choice

Let butter reach room temperature. Combine all ingredients. Whip together until light and fluffy.

QUICK FRUIT LOAF

A favorite quick bread that can be made any time of the year. Use fresh cherries in season or substitute frozen or canned if out of season; delicious either way! We have even served it instead of the traditional fruitcake around the holidays. Even quicker when made in your food processor. Makes 1 loaf.

1 1/2 cups all-purpose flour, sifted
1 Tbsp. baking powder (regular or low-sodium)
1/2 cup granulated sugar
1/2 cup (1 stick) butter **or** margarine
2 eggs, beaten **or** equivalent egg substitute
2 Tbsp. **Cherry Liqueur or** other fruit liqueur
1 cup pitted cherries, fresh, frozen or canned*
1/3 cup raisins
2/3 cup mixed dried fruit

Preheat oven to 350° F.

Place flour, baking powder and sugar in a large mixing or food processor bowl. Mix dry ingredients. Cut butter into chunks and add to flour mixture. Cut in butter with pastry cutter or pulse with steel blade until mixture resembles coarse bread crumbs. If using food processor, remove mixture at this time and place in large bowl. Add eggs and liqueur; mix gently. Fold in all fruits.

Spray, with vegetable coating spray, or grease an 8 1/2 " x 4 1/2 " x 2 1/2 " loaf pan. Pour mixture into pan. Bake for 55 to 60 minutes.

Test baked loaf with a wooden toothpick in the center. Will test clean when done. Remove from oven and let cool for 10 to 15 minutes before removing from pan. Serve plain or drizzle with Liqueur Glaze, before serving.

* If using canned cherries, drain well before adding to mixture.

AMARETTO-ALMOND TEA CAKE

*This moist and perfectly yummy cake contains the wonderful ingredients that made **Amaretto Liqueur** famous: almonds and apricots. The liqueur itself adds a flavorful note to the cake and a richness to the special glaze. Just for fun, hide a whole almond in the batter before baking. The fortunate finder will have the best of luck for the next year!*

Cake:

1 cup butter **or** margarine
1 1/3 cups granulated sugar
4 eggs
1/2 tsp. almond extract
1 cup lemon yogurt
2 1/2 cups all-purpose flour
1 tsp. baking powder
1 tsp. baking soda
1 cup finely chopped, blanched almonds
1 whole shelled almond (optional)

Drizzle:

1 Tbsp. **Amaretto Liqueur**

Glaze and Decoration:

2/3 cup apricot jam
2 Tbsp. **Amaretto Liqueur**
3/4 cup finely chopped, blanched almonds
3/4 cup whole blanched almonds (optional)

Preheat oven to 350°F. Generously grease an 8" to 9" springform pan. Cut a circle of waxed paper to fit the bottom of the pan; place it in the pan and grease the paper. Flour the pan.

Cream butter or margarine. Add the sugar and cream well. Beat in 1 egg at a time, until all are combined. Stir in the almond extract and yogurt. Add the dry ingredients, beating well. Mix in the 1 cup chopped almonds. Pour into the prepared pan, press the whole almond into the batter (if desired) and bake for 50 to 60 minutes, until cake tester comes out clean.

Cool in pan for 10 minutes; remove sides of pan and cool to lukewarm. Pierce top of cake with a fork at 1" intervals, to a depth of 1/4". Drizzle liqueur over the surface of the cooled cake.

Force apricot jam through a wire mesh strainer to obtain a smooth textured glaze or process in a food processor or blender. Add the 2 tablespoons Amaretto, mixing well to combine. Spoon three-fourths of the glaze over the top and sides of the cake, covering the surface completely. Press the chopped almonds to the sides of the cake and decorate the top with whole almonds in a starburst pattern or a design of your choice. Spoon the remaining glaze over the top decoration.

Variation: Almond Layer Cake - Increase the apricot jam to 1 cup and combine this with 2 tablespoons plus 2 teaspoons Amaretto Liqueur, for the glaze. With a long knife, carefully split the cooled, undecorated cake into 2 layers. Drizzle each layer with 2 teaspoons Amaretto. Spread a layer of the glaze over one layer of cake and top with the second cake layer. Glaze and decorate according to directions above.

APPLE PIE SNACK CAKE

The heady aroma of this fall and winter favorite has filled the air at so many of our cooking classes. This moist, "anytime" cake is especially welcome when the air is crisp. It's an easy-to-make recipe you'll love. Bake it fresh or make it ahead and reheat slightly to serve. A sturdy cake that can be frozen for later use or gift-giving. Makes two 9" cakes.

Dry Ingredients:

1 3/4 cups granulated sugar
2 1/2 cups cake flour
1/2 cup golden seedless raisins
1 tsp. ground cinnamon
1/4 tsp. ground cloves
1/2 tsp. ground allspice
1 1/2 tsp. baking soda
1/2 tsp. baking powder
1/2 tsp. salt, (optional)
1/8 tsp. instant coffee
   Vanilla Sugar **or** confectioners' sugar

Liquid Ingredients:

2 eggs
1/2 cup spiced **or** unspiced **Apple Liqueur**
2/3 cup cooking oil
2 cups apple pie filling

Preheat oven to 350° F. Grease and flour or spray with vegetable coating, two round or square 9" cake pans. Combine all dry ingredients in a large mixing bowl; mix well.

In a medium mixing bowl, beat eggs. Add rest of liquid ingredients; stir well until combined. Pour liquid ingredients into dry ingredients. Beat well to completely mix, scraping sides occasionally. Pour into prepared pans. Bake for 50 to 55 minutes. Test with toothpick for doneness. Cool in pans on cake racks.

When cooled, sprinkle with Vanilla Sugar, (see page 107).

CITRUS LIQUEUR CAKE

A heavy, old-fashioned type of cake that is wonderful made with any citrus flavors. Match the grated rind with the dominant flavor in the liqueur of choice, i.e.: **Orange Liqueur** *and grated orange rind. Serve plain or topped with* **Liqueur Glaze** *or whipped cream . Makes one large tube or bundt cake.*

Cake:

3 1/2 cups cake flour
2 tsp. baking soda
1 Tbsp. fresh grated citrus rind, flavor of choice
1 cup, (2 sticks) butter **or** margarine
1 1/2 cups granulated sugar
4 eggs
1 1/3 cups buttermilk
3/4 cup chopped walnuts
3/4 cup raisins
2 Tbsp. **Taboo or** a citrus liqueur of choice

Preheat oven to 350° F. Grease or spray with vegetable coating , an 8" tube or bundt pan. Set aside.

Plump raisins by pouring boiling water over, covering completely. Let sit 10 minutes. Drain off all water. Pour liqueur over raisins and set aside until needed.

In a large mixing bowl, cream butter with sugar. Add one egg at a time until well mixed, scraping sides of the bowl with a spatula as needed. Add baking soda to butter mixture, stirring well. Alternate additions of flour and buttermilk to the mixture. Stir in walnuts, liqueured raisins and grated orange rind.

Pour mixture into prepared pan. Bake about 50 minutes or until cake tests done with a toothpick. Remove from oven, let cool a bit then poke cake with toothpick. Pour Citrus Drizzle over.

Citrus Liqueur Drizzle:
1/2 cup orange **or** citrus juice
1/4 cup **Taboo or** a citrus liqueur of choice

91

CRÈME DE MENTHE FROSTING

*A luscious and easy-to-make frosting that makes brownies or chocolate cake very, very special. Authors Joyce Webster and Susan Vander Velde shared this versatile recipe with us. It's from their cookbook, **Try It, You'll Like It! Microwave Desserts.** If you don't have a microwave oven, use a double boiler to make the chocolate glaze. Makes enough to frost a 9" cake.*

1/3 cup butter
1 1/2 cups confectioners' sugar
1 Tbsp. corn syrup
2 Tbsp. **Crème de Menthe Liqueur***
1/2 tsp. vanilla extract

Chocolate Glaze:

1/2 cup chocolate chips
1 Tbsp. butter
1 Tbsp. milk

In a 4-cup measure combine butter, sugar, corn syrup, Crème de Menthe and vanilla. Stir until smooth and creamy.

In a separate measure combine chocolate chips and butter. Microwave uncovered, on **HIGH (100%)** power for 1 minute or until chocolate has melted. (Stir to test melting.) Stir in milk until smooth.

Spread Crème de Menthe frosting over top of brownies or cake. Drizzle melted chocolate in a criss-cross fashion over frosting. Refrigerate.

*Note: Fresh Mint or **Dutch Chocolate-Mint Liqueurs** may be substituted for the Crème De Menthe Liqueur in this recipe.

ITALIAN ANISE STARS

These tiny, buttery, melt-in-your-mouth stars have just the merest tantalizing hint of Anisette. Makes 9 dozen tiny stars.

1 cup butter
1/3 cup golden brown sugar
2 1/4 cups all-purpose flour
2 Tbsp. **Anisette Liqueur**

Preheat oven to 325° F. In a mixing bowl, cream the butter; add the sugar gradually, combining thoroughly. Mix in half of the flour until dough is smooth, then add the liqueur, beating until well blended.

Sprinkle the remaining flour over a pastry cloth or smooth rolling surface until the excess flour has been worked into the dough. Refrigerate dough at least one hour for easier handling.

On a lightly floured surface, roll dough to 1/4" thickness. Use a 1 3/4" cookie cutter dipped in flour to cut the tiny star-shaped cookies. Transfer to an ungreased baking sheet; bake for 12 minutes or until just the edges are a light golden brown.

Variation: For a moist cookie with a more pronounced anise flavor, brush the tops of the stars while still hot, with a glaze made from one teaspoon granulated sugar combined with 2 teaspoons **Anisette Liqueur**.

LIQUEUR GLAZE

So useful for a quick glaze, drizzle or use as a special topping on many baked items. Makes about 1/4 cup.

1/2 cup confectioners' sugar
3 1/2 tsp. liqueur of choice

Place ingredients in a small bowl. Combine and beat with a whisk or beater until smooth.

CHOCOLATE ORANGE FONDUE

Fantastically quick and sinfully good! A "must do" recipe! Dip assorted fresh fruits into this fondue or use as a warm sauce over ice cream or frozen yogurt. Refrigerates and reheats well. Makes over 1 cup.

1/2 cup whipping cream
2 Tbsp. **Orange Liqueur,** any type
2 bars (4-ounces each) German chocolate, broken into pieces

Combine all ingredients and cook in a double boiler, stirring constantly, until smooth and satiny. Serve warm.

Microwave Directions:
In a 1-quart or larger glass bowl combine cream and liqueur. Add chocolate pieces. Microwave on **MEDIUM-HIGH (70%)** for 2 1/2 to 3 minutes , stirring halfway through cooking time. Remove from microwave oven. Stir or whisk until smooth. If some chunks remain add more time, 15 seconds at a time. Stir again.

CHOCOLATE NUT RUFFLE

Any cookbook worth its salt has at least one very special recipe. This is it! We have had more compliments on this dessert than we can count. A caterer selected this recipe and served it to a conference of over 250 Librarians. (Our library book sales went up dramatically!) We can only say, if you like chocolate, do try it. Rich and wonderful, it is pretty served in demitasse cups or small, footed glasses. Makes 8 demitasse servings.

1 cup superfine **or** regular granulated sugar
3/4 cup cocoa powder (fine Dutch cocoa preferred)
1/2 cup **Old Jamaican Coffee Liqueur**
4 egg yolks
1 cup whipping cream
1/2 cup chopped almonds, toasted
3/4 cup coarsely chopped semi-sweet chocolate
    semi-sweet chocolate shavings for garnish

In the top portion of a double boiler, combine the sugar, cocoa and liqueur. Cook over medium heat 15 minutes, stirring constantly.

In a large bowl, beat the egg yolks until slightly fluffy, about 1 to 2 minutes. Slowly drizzle the hot chocolate mixture into the beaten yolks, beating to combine. Beat for 2 minutes more, scraping sides of bowl as needed. Refrigerate until cold (30 to 45 minutes).

Whip cream until stiff peaks form. Add a spoonful of whipped cream to the chocolate mixture and stir in to soften the chocolate. Fold in the remainder of the whipped cream, very gently. Add almonds and chopped chocolate, stirring just enough to combine. Be careful not to disturb the fluffiness of the whipped cream.

The mixture may be frozen at this point. Cover bowl or fill cups or glasses with mixture, allowing about 1/2 cup per serving. Garnish with chocolate shavings and cover and freeze. Freeze at least 2 hours before serving. Serve frozen.

CHOCOLATE-LOVERS' COOKIE PIECRUST

*There are so many uses for this wonderful easy-to-make crust. Try it with **Ice Cream Social Pie** to start. Makes one 9" piecrust.*

20 cream-filled chocolate sandwich cookies
3 Tbsp. melted butter or margarine
1 Tbsp. liqueur of choice*

Preheat oven to 350° F. Crush cookies by hand or in a food processor with a steel knife, until fine.

Pour cookie crumbs into a 9" pie plate and drizzle with melted butter. Stir well to combine. Pat evenly to cover bottom and sides of pie plate. Bake for 10 to 12 minutes. Let cool slightly; drizzle liqueur over crust. Fill or refrigerate until ready to use.

Microwave Directions: Microwave crust on **HIGH (100%)** power for 2 to 2 1/2 minutes, quarter turning halfway through cooking time. Proceed as directed.

***Liqueur Choices:** Some liqueurs that are excellent in this recipe are **Dutch Chocolate-Mint, Fresh Mint, Crème de Menthe, Amaretto, Italian Hazelnut, Mexican Coffee** or **Old Jamaican Coffee.**

GOURMET FUDGE SAUCE

*Use on **Ice Cream Social Pie** or make wonderful gourmet ice cream sundaes. The use of the food processor makes this recipe a snap. Makes about 3/4 cup.*

4 oz. semi-sweet chocolate
1/3 cup granulated sugar
2 Tbsp. butter or margarine
1/4 cup water
2 Tbsp. liqueur of choice*

Insert steel knife/blade in food processor. Break chocolate blocks into smaller pieces. Turn processor on and drop pieces, one at a time, through feed tube. Process until finely minced.

Heat water and butter; stir in sugar. When sugar has dissolved, remove from heat and pour through feed tube with processor motor running. Add liqueur last. Sauce is ready for use.

*Liqueur Choices:** Some liqueurs that are excellent in this recipe are **Dutch Chocolate-Mint, Fresh Mint, Crème de Menthe, Amaretto, Italian Hazelnut, Mexican Coffee , Old Jamaican Coffee,** or **Orange.**

ICE CREAM SOCIAL PIE

This pie has a rich, old-fashioned taste but is easy-to-make and freezes beautifully for "make-ahead" entertaining. Makes one 9" pie.

Fill **Chocolate-Lovers Cookie Piecrust** with:

1 1/2 qts. French Vanilla **or** favorite flavor ice cream

Place ice cream in scoops, slightly mounding up in the center. Set in freezer while making Gourmet Fudge Sauce (page 96).

When fudge sauce is made pour over frozen ice cream pie. Replace in freezer. Whipped Liqueur Cream (page 107) or conventional whipped cream may be used to garnish this pie. Red or green maraschino cherries and/or chopped nuts also make nice additions to this dessert.

Note: To make pie ahead, cover with plastic wrap or aluminum foil as soon as fudge sauce has firmed in freezer. Add whipped cream just before serving.

97

DUTCH LAWYERS' PIE

A coconut crust, creamy filling with a surprise center layer combine to make this a spectacular pie! Makes one 9" pie.

1/4 cup melted butter **or** margarine
2 2/3 cups flaked sweetened coconut
1/2 cup granulated sugar
1 envelope (1 Tablespoon) unflavored gelatin
3 eggs, separated
3/4 cup milk
1/2 cup **Advocaat Liqueur**
1 cup whipping cream
1 tsp. vanilla extract
1/2 tsp. lemon extract
    whipped cream for garnish, if desired

Crust: Preheat oven to 325° F. In a medium saucepan, melt butter; stir in flaked coconut. Press half of this mixture over bottom and sides of a 9" pie plate. Spread remainder on a baking sheet. Bake both for 10 to 15 minutes, or until coconut is golden brown. (Watch closely! The coconut on the baking sheet may cook more quickly than the crust.) Remove from oven and let cool.

Filling: In medium saucepan, combine 1/4 cup of the sugar, the gelatin, egg yolks and milk. Stir constantly over medium-low heat, until gelatin and sugar are dissolved. Cool to lukewarm; stir in the liqueur. Refrigerate until mixture is thick but not set.

In small mixing bowl, beat egg whites until soft peaks form. Add the remaining 1/4 cup sugar gradually, while beating until stiff peaks form. Set aside.

In a medium bowl, whip cream until stiff; gradually add vanilla and lemon extracts. Fold the cream gently into the gelatin mixture, then fold in the beaten egg whites. Refrigerate until mixture holds its shape when mounded. Spoon half the filling into cooled crust. Layer with most of the toasted coconut. Top with remaining filling. Chill until set. Garnish with whipped cream and remaining toasted coconut. Serve chilled.

ELEGANT BERRY WHIP

Serve icy cold in stemmed glasses. A wide variety of berries may be used with this recipe. Raspberries and strawberries are two favorites. Serves 6.

2 cups (1 pint) fresh berries
1 cup whipping cream
1/2 cup sifted confectioners' sugar
1 egg white
1 Tbsp. liqueur of choice*

Prepare berries; wash, remove hulls, etc. Set aside 6 whole, perfect berries. Place remaining berries in blender or food processor and purée.

Whip cream until soft peaks form, then beat in sugar. Beat egg white until stiff. Fold beaten egg white gently into fruit purée. Fold purée mixture into cream mixture. Spoon into six individual dishes or stemmed glasses. Chill well. Garnish with reserved berries.

*Raspberry, Strawberry, Lemon, or **Amaretto Liqueurs** are very good in this recipe.

ELEGANT CHOCOLATE CREPES

'Elegant' is the only word to describe this rich, French-inspired dessert. Serves 10 lucky people, two crêpes each.

2 Tbsp. powdered cocoa (Dutch preferred)
1 cup sifted all-purpose flour
1/2 cup confectioners' sugar
4 eggs
1 cup milk
1/2 tsp. vanilla
2 Tbsp. melted butter **or** margarine
  sweetened whipped cream
3/4 cup **Crème de Cacao Liqueur**

Sift flour and cocoa into a medium mixing bowl. Stir in sugar and set aside.

Beat eggs until thick and lemon-colored. Stir in milk, vanilla and melted butter. Whisk egg mixture into flour mixture. Beat until batter is smooth. Let batter stand one hour for better crêpes.

Heat crêpe or omelet pan over medium-low heat. Brush with cooking oil. Pour a small amount of batter into pan. Swirl pan so batter thinly coats the bottom. Cook until crêpe is set and edges dry. Gently turn crêpe over with spatula. Cook briefly on second side. Remove crêpe and repeat.

When serving immediately, place crêpes directly onto serving plate(s), folding each into quarters. Hold in warming oven until all are prepared. If making ahead, place crêpe on lightly-oiled waxed paper (use a brush to oil the paper). Top with another piece of oiled paper; repeat. Wrap stack of crêpes in aluminium foil and store in refrigerator or freezer until ready to use.

To reheat, loosen foil and place on a cookie sheet. Bake in a low oven, 275° F, until warm.

Whip cream and sweeten to taste. Place two crêpes on serving plate, top with dollop of whipped cream and drizzle 2 tablespoons of liqueur over each serving. Serve immediately.

LIQUEUR GLAZED NUTS

*A special treat alone or use to top a gourmet sundae or cake. Experiment with your favorite liqueur flavors to see which you like the most. Two of our favorites to begin with are **Orange** and **Amaretto Liqueurs**. Fast and easy in the microwave oven. Makes about 1/2 cup.*

1/2 cup blanched nuts (almonds, filberts, etc.)
3 Tbsp. liqueur of choice

Pour liqueur into a 9" glass pie plate. Add nuts and stir to coat very well. Microwave on **HIGH (100%)** power for 4 minutes, or until glazed and a light golden brown. Important: stir every minute.

The nuts will continue to toast after cooking. Spread on plastic wrap or aluminium foil after nuts have cooled a minute or two. Cool further. Wrap up or store in an airtight container.

LIGHT RASPBERRY FROST

An elegant and light dessert. Refreshingly perfect! Serve in chilled stemmed glasses. Makes five 1/2 cup servings.

1 (10 oz.) pkg. sweetened frozen raspberries, thawed
1 Tbsp. cornstarch
1/4 cup confectioners' sugar
1/4 cup **Raspberry Liqueur**
few additional fresh **or** frozen berries

Place a small strainer over a glass measuring cup. Drain juice off raspberries through strainer. Measure juice; add water, if necessary, to equal 1/2 cup. Combine 2 tablespoons juice and cornstarch in a small bowl; set aside.

In a small saucepan combine remaining juice and sugar. Cook over low heat, stirring to dissolve sugar. Add reserved cornstarch mixture and continue stirring until mixture is thick and clear. Add Raspberry Liqueur and stir in thawed berries. Spoon into serving dishes. Top with additional berries if desired.

Microwave Directions: To quickly thaw frozen berries, place unopened paper box on plate and microwave on **DEFROST** (**30%**) power for 3 to 5 minutes, let stand 5 minutes. If top and bottom of container are metal, remove top as directed and place container, open side up, on a plate and microwave as directed.

Follow recipe directions, but combine juice and sugar in a microwave-safe medium mixing bowl. Microwave on **HIGH** (**100%**) power for 1 1/2 minutes, stirring once.

Add cornstarch mixture, stirring in well. Continue microwaving on **HIGH** for 2 to 3 minutes, stirring every minute, until mixture is thick and clear. Follow remaining directions above.

MELON SORBET

*A refreshing and light sorbet with just a touch of liqueur from
one of our favorite cooks, Janice Kenyon. She is the author of*
Light Fantastic: Health-Conscious Entertaining.
Serves 6 to 8.

Purée in food processor:
chunks of 4 small or 3 medium cantalope or other sweet melon,
peeled and seeded, enough to make about 4 cups purée.
(Save some melon balls for garnish.)

Add:
1/2 cup water
3 Tbsp. honey
juice of 1 lime
2 Tbsp. fruit liqueur, preferably **Raspberry Liqueur**

Garnish:
melon balls, same or different type of melon
strawberries (optional)
kiwi fruit slices (optional)

Pour into 2 freezer trays or 9"x9" baking pan and freeze until
firm, about 1 hour. Remove from freezer, break into chunks and
process in food processor until smooth. Freeze again and repeat
blending process two more times (an ice cream maker does these
steps automatically). Transfer from freezer to refrigerator while
dinner is being served.

To serve, scoop into small serving bowls over a few melon balls
(another kind of melon for contrast if desired), and garnish with
a whole strawberry and/or slice of kiwi fruit.

QUICK BLUEBERRY DELIGHT

A simple dessert or brunch dish that is quick to prepare and delightful to eat. Serves 1; increase as needed for quanity.

1/2 cup fresh **or** thawed frozen blueberries
1 Tbsp. **Orange Liqueur** (any type)
1 heaping Tbsp. whipped cream **or Whipped Liqueur Cream**

In dessert bowl place washed, drained blueberries. Spoon liqueur over berries and let stand at least 5 minutes. Top with whipped cream of choice just before serving.

STRAWBERRY ICE

*This easy, light and luscious recipe can be made with any of our **Orange Liqueurs**. Fellow author Janice Kenyon shares this outstanding example of a liqueur-enhanced dessert from her **Light Fantastic: Health Conscious Entertaining** cookbook. Serves 4 to 6.*

Purée in blender or food processor:
2 cups sliced strawberries, fresh or thawed frozen
1 Tbsp. lemon juice

In medium saucepan combine purée with:
1 3/4 cups water
1/2 cup sugar

Heat to boiling and boil slowly until frothy, about 5 minutes. Add:
3 Tbsp. **Orange Liqueur**

Pour into freezer tray and freeze until slushy firm, about 2 hours. Remove from freezer tray, beat to break up chunks if necessary, then fold in:
1 stiffly beaten egg white

Return to freezer until firm, about 1 hour. Serve garnished with sliced berries or kiwi fruit.

STEAMED ORANGE PUDDING

Moist, cake-like steamed puddings have long been an English and Canadian favorite. Make them without any special steaming equipment using our "oven-steaming" method that saves time too. Try this homey, old-fashioned dessert served warm and topped with a custard sauce or our special **California Lemon Sauce**. *Serves 6.*

1/2 cup Sultana raisins
1/4 cup dark raisins
1/4 cup any type of **Orange Liqueur**
1 cup dry breadcrumbs
3/4 cup all-purpose flour
1/3 cup brown sugar
1/2 cup granulated sugar
1 tsp. freshly grated orange peel
1/2 tsp. freshly grated lemon peel
1 tsp. baking soda
1/4 cup scalded milk
1/4 cup cold milk
1 beaten egg
1/2 cup (1 stick) butter **or** margarine, melted
2 to 3 Tbsp. any type of **Orange Liqueur**

Preheat oven to 375° F. Measure raisins; pour the 1/4 cup liqueur over them. Set aside until needed.

Mix bread crumbs, flour, sugars, orange and lemon peels in a large mixing bowl, stirring until well mixed.

Stir baking soda into the scalded milk, then add remaining milk. Stir in melted butter and beaten egg. Pour into crumb-flour mixture; mixing well. Stir in the raisin-liqueur mixture.

Butter a 1-quart baking dish. Spoon batter into dish. Cover with aluminium foil, sealing down all around. Pour about 3/4" of water into a cake pan; place the 1-quart baking dish into cake pan. Set carefully into oven. Bake 1 1/4 hours. Test center with a toothpick (will come out clean when done).

TRUFFLES

*Rich chocolate and a mellow liqueur make an unbeatable combination in this special truffle recipe. Try **Mexican Coffee** or **Old Jamaican Coffee Liqueurs** for Mocha Truffles. Other flavors that are heavenly with chocolate are **Cherry, Orange, Raspberry, Hazelnut** or **Mint Liqueurs**. You'll discover many favorites in this versatile recipe. Makes 1 1/2 dozen large truffles.*

12 oz. semi-sweet chocolate, either chips **or** broken into pieces
4 Tbsp. (1/2 stick) butter **or** margarine
1/4 cup granulated sugar
2 egg yolks, beaten
1 cup finely chopped nuts, (hazelnuts, pecans, walnuts **or** blanched almonds)
1/3 cup liqueur of choice
Coating choice of: chocolate decorettes, unsweetened **or** presweetened cocoa powder

Heat water in the bottom part of a double boiler. Place chocolate in the top half of the double boiler and stir until melted. Gradually stir in the butter. Add sugar and continue to cook, stirring constantly until sugar is dissolved. Remove from heat and allow to cool as much as possible without letting chocolate harden.

Quickly stir in the beaten egg yolks. Add nuts and mix well. Stir in liqueur. Refrigerate 15 minutes or until mixture is easily handled and not sticky.

Place a small amount of your choice of coating in a small bowl. Shape refrigerated mixture into large balls (about 1 1/4"). Roll in coating. Chill until very firm.

VANILLA SUGAR

Excellent for desserts, coffees and confections. A good way to make full use of expensive vanilla beans used in liqueur making. Makes 1 pint.

Rinse vanilla beans in cool water to remove any liqueur. Place on a doubled paper towel and pat tops dry with another paper towel. Let dry completely.

When dry, place in a pint jar with two cups granulated sugar, cap and shake well. Let age at least a few days before using.

WHIPPED LIQUEUR CREAM

Use on Ice Cream Social Pie or any other recipe where a very special whipped cream is called for. Vary flavors to suit your recipe. Makes about 1 pint of whipped cream.

1/2 pt. whipping cream
2 to 3 Tbsp. confectioners' sugar
1 Tbsp. liqueur of choice

Whip cream until soft peaks form. Add sugar; whip a bit more. Add liqueur and whip lightly to combine. Serve or chill, covered, until needed.

GERMAN APPLE PANCAKE PUFF

This recipe is a cook's dream. It's quick, easy to prepare, economical, absolutely delicious and a guaranteed "showstopper". Try it as an entrée for a special brunch, breakfast or late supper. Serves 3 to 4.

3 apples, peeled, cored and sliced
3 Tbsp. **Apple Liqueur**, spiced **or** unspiced
6 eggs, separated
1/4 cup all-purpose flour
1/4 cup melted butter **or** margarine
1/4 cup rich milk **or** half-and-half
2 Tbsp. butter or margarine

Topping:
4 Tbsp. sugar
1 tsp. ground cinnamon

Combine topping ingredients. Set aside.

Preheat oven to 400° F. Place apples in medium mixing bowl. Pour liqueur over apples and stir gently to coat. Let stand while preparing pancake.

Beat egg yolks; mix in flour, melted butter and milk. Beat egg whites until they form stiff peaks. Fold beaten egg whites into flour mixture.

Heat 2 tablespoons butter in a large oven-proof skillet. When butter is melted, tilt pan to coat bottom and sides; pour in pancake batter. Spoon liqueured apples over top of batter to within 1/2" of edge.

Cook over medium heat for approximately 5 minutes. Transfer skillet to oven and bake for 15 minutes or until golden brown. Top with cinnamon-sugar topping mixture, cut into wedges and serve hot.

MANDARIN YAM BAKE

Tired of the traditional marshmallow/sweet potato dishes? We are! This recipe is guaranteed not to have a marshmallow in it, and is quite different and delicious. Serves 8.

5 cups (40-oz. can) cooked yams **or** sweet potatoes, peeled, drained and mashed
1/4 cup melted butter **or** margarine
1/3 cup **Taboo Liqueur**
1 small can (11-oz.) drained mandarin oranges
1/4 cup chopped macadamia nuts, pecans **or** walnuts
1/3 cup firmly packed brown sugar
1 Tbsp. butter **or** margarine

Preheat oven to 375° F. Combine mashed yams, 1/4 cup melted butter and Taboo Liqueur in a 2-quart casserole dish; mix well. Gently fold in drained mandarin orange sections. Pat down evenly in casserole. Sprinkle brown sugar and nuts over top of casserole and dot with the one tablespoon of butter. Bake for 30 minutes.

Microwave Directions: Cover microwave-safe dish with waxed paper. Cook on **HIGH (100%)** power for 7 to 8 minutes. Quarter turn dish halfway through cooking time, as necessary. Let rest, covered, 5 minutes for carry-over cooking before serving.

PLUM GLAZED CORNISH HENS

Our cooking school favorite is wonderful for entertaining. Make with Cornish game hens, pheasant, whole or cut-up chicken. Serve with wild rice or a rice pilaf. Serves 4 to 8.

4 Cornish game hens **or** 2 roaster/fryer chickens
  Salt or substitute salt (optional)
  Dash white pepper
4 to 8 tiny onions, peeled
1 1/2 cups pitted canned plums
1/4 cup reserved plum juice
1 1/2 Tbsp. cornstarch
1/4 cup raisins
3 Tbsp. sugar
2 Tbsp. lemon juice
1 1/2 Tbsp. onion powder
1/2 cup **Plum Liqueur**

Prepare poultry. Remove giblets from center cavity. Wash, pat dry. Lightly salt and pepper cavity. Place 1 to 4 onions inside each cavity. Tie legs together with string. Arrange in baking dish and set aside while making sauce.

Purée pitted plums in processor or blender. Combine cornstarch and reserved plum juice in a small bowl, mix well. Pour all ingredients except raisins and liqueur in a small saucepan. Heat to a beginning boil and simmer until slightly thickened, stirring constantly. Remove from heat and stir in liqueur and raisins.

Pour sauce over game hens. Cover and bake at 350° F about 1 1/2 hours. Baste halfway through cooking and again near end.

Tip: Decrease time to about 1 hour if using poultry parts. Check doneness.

Clay Pot Directions: *An alternate method of cooking.*
Soak empty clay pot and cover in lukewarm water for 15 minutes. Drain off excess water by placing on clean toweling for a few minutes. Place poultry in pot. Pour sauce over and cover. Place clay pot in a *cold* unheated oven. Turn oven to 425°F. Bake 1 to 1 1/4 hours. Baste near end of cooking time.

ROAST PORK WITH DANISH CHERRY SAUCE

Pork roast is a classic Danish dish, often served at a special dinner. The spicy Cherry Sauce is the crowning touch to this dish. Conventional oven and microwave cooking directions are given. Serve with tiny oven browned potatoes. Serves 6 to 8.

Roast:

4 1/2 to 5 lbs. center cut pork loin roast (boneless **or** bone-in)
1/2 tsp. pepper

Preheat oven to 350° F. Lightly pepper pork loin on all sides. Place roast, fat side up, on roasting rack in open shallow roasting pan. Allow 30 to 35 minutes per pound and roast at 350° F until roast reaches an internal temperature of 165° F. (Test with a meat thermometer in the meaty center of the roast.) Remove from oven and let stand 15 to 20 minutes before serving. (Make sauce at this time.)

Sauce:

1/2 cup red cherry preserves
1/4 cup white corn syrup
1 Tbsp. white **or** white wine vinegar
1/4 cup **Cherry Liqueur**
1/8 tsp. ground cinnamon
1/8 tsp. ground cloves

Combine all ingredients, except two tablespoons liqueur, in a saucepan. Bring to a gentle boil and simmer for 1 minute. Remove from heat and stir in remaining liqueur. Spoon all or part over roast before serving. Serve with extra sauce, if any, on the side.

Microwave Directions:

Lightly pepper pork loin on all sides. Place fat side down on a microwave roasting rack in a 2 quart or larger glass baking dish. Microwave on **HIGH (100%)** power for 20 minutes. Next, turn roast fat side up. Microwave on **MEDIUM-HIGH (70%)** power for about 15 to 20 minutes or until center of meat reaches 160° F. (Be sure to use only a microwave meat thermometer or probe if checking temperature inside an operating microwave oven.) Remove from oven and place a loose tent of aluminium foil or a microwave roast cover over roast and let stand for 15 to 20 minutes before serving.

Sauce:

Combine all ingredients except 2 tablespoons Cherry Liqueur in a 2-cup glass measure. Microwave on **HIGH (100%)** power for 3 minutes. Stir in remaining liqueur. Serve as previously directed.

AMARETTO APPLESAUCE

A fresh sauce that is excellent over gingerbread or as a filling for dessert crêpes. Top with a dusting of confectioners' sugar, sour or whipped cream for a finishing touch! Wonderful with pork too. Microwave cooking experts Joyce Webster and Susan Vander Velde share this from their great dessert cookbook, Try It, You'll Like It! Microwaved Desserts. Makes 2 cups.

4 apples, peeled and cored
2 Tbsp. butter
1/2 cup sugar
1 tsp. grated orange rind
2 Tbsp. orange juice
1 egg, separated
2 Tbsp. **Amaretto Liqueur**

Chop apples and combine with butter, sugar, orange rind and juice in a 4 cup mixing bowl. Cook conventionally until apples are tender or microwave on **HIGH (100%)** power for 5 minutes, uncovered. Stir once or twice. Purée apples in food processor or blender.

Beat egg yolk and liqueur together. Add to applesauce. Whip egg white until stiff. Gradually blend into applesauce.

CALIFORNIA LEMON SAUCE

A bright and sunny sauce that has so many uses. Wonderful over plum pudding, gingerbread, pound cake or our Steamed Orange Pudding. Makes about 1 cup.

3/4 cup water
1/2 cup granulated sugar
2 Tbsp. cornstarch
1 Tbsp. butter
1/4 cup lemon juice, fresh preferred
2 tsp. grated fresh lemon rind
1 egg, beaten
2 Tbsp. **Lemon Liqueur**

Bring water to a boil. In a small saucepan, combine sugar and cornstarch. Gradually stir in boiling water. Boil 1 minute, stirring constantly.

Remove from heat and stir in butter, lemon juice and rind. Gradually blend in egg and finally liqueur. Serve slightly warm or cool.

CRANBERRY JEWELS IN LIQUEUR

The colors are beautiful in this memorable side dish that is especially good with poultry. Makes about 1 quart.

1 cup granulated sugar
1/2 cup orange juice
2 cups cranberries
1 can (11 ozs.) mandarin oranges, well drained
1/4 cup **Orange Liqueur**, any type

Combine sugar and orange juice in a large saucepan. Cook over medium heat, about 3 to 4 minutes, stirring occasionally until sugar dissolves. Stir in cranberries. Heat to boiling point then reduce heat. Simmer uncovered until juice is released from cranberries, about 10 minutes. Add liqueur and mandarin oranges; simmer 2 minutes. Pour into container, cool, cover and refrigerate. Serve chilled.

Microwave Directions:

In a 1 1/2 to 2-quart microwavable bowl, combine cranberries, sugar and orange juice. Cover and microwave on **HIGH (100%)** power for 3 minutes. Stir and microwave for 2 to 3 minutes more, or until cranberries have popped their skins. Let stand covered, for 5 minutes. Gently stir in liqueur and drained mandarin oranges. Cover and refrigerate. Serve chilled.

LIQUEURED FRUIT SAUCE

A quick, easy and gourmet sauce that can be spooned over almost anything! Makes even plain pound cake, bread pudding or vanilla ice cream sing! A good make-ahead recipe. Makes about 3/4 cup.

1 tsp. fresh orange **or** lemon zest
1 cup apricot **or** peach preserves
5 Tbsp. **Apricot** or **Peach Liqueur**, divided

Combine zest, preserves and 2 tablespoons liqueur in a small saucepan. Heat to a boil, stirring constantly. Reduce heat and simmer gently for about 10 minutes, stirring frequently. Remove from heat and stir in 3 tablespoons liqueur. Serve slightly warm.

ORIENTAL PLUM SAUCE

*Another one of our students' cooking class favorites. It is an exotic cousin of Sweet and Sour sauce. Its rich, fruity taste combines plums and apricots with the added pizazz of **Orange Liqueur**.*

*Choose any of the **Orange Liqueurs** , including **Taboo,** in this book; all are successful in this recipe. Serve with meats or poultry. Especially good as a dipping sauce for fried won ton, Chinese chicken wings or egg rolls. Makes about 1 1/2 cups.*

1/4 cup dried apricots
  boiling water
1 cup fresh **or** frozen pitted red **or** purple plums*
2 Tbsp. water **or** plum juice
1/2 cup granulated sugar*
1/2 tsp. dry powdered mustard
1/8 tsp white **or** black pepper
1/4 cup white vinegar
1/4 cup **Orange Liqueur**

Cover dried apricots with boiling water and let stand 10 minutes. Drain and finely chop apricots by hand or in a food processor with a steel knife/blade. Finely chop plums. Place fruit in a medium saucepan; add the 2 tablespoons water or juice. Bring just to a boil, lower heat and simmer for 15 minutes, stirring frequently.

Add sugar, mustard and pepper. Simmer for 10 minutes. Stir in vinegar. Simmer 5 minutes. Remove from heat and cool to lukewarm. Stir in liqueur. Serve at room temperature or slightly warmed.

Microwave Directions: Prepare fruit as directed. Omit any additional water from recipe. Place fruit in a small glass mixing bowl and microwave on **HIGH (100%)** power, stirring after 2 minutes; stir. Reduce power to **MEDIUM-LOW (50%)** power and simmer 5 minutes. Stir every minute.

Add sugar and spices, mixing well. Simmer for 4 minutes on **MEDIUM-LOW** power, stirring after 2 minutes. Let cool and stir in liqueur. Serve as directed.

*Note: One 16-ounce can of drained and pitted purple plums may be substituted for the fresh or frozen plums. Decrease sugar to 1/4 cup; check consistency, water or juice may not be necessary.

HIGHLAND MARMALADE

*Put some of this marmalade on a hot scone, take a bite and close your eyes. You can almost feel the Scottish mist curl at your feet and smell the heather in bloom. Top a jar with a piece of tartan fabric for a perfect gift to any marmalade or **Drambuie** lover. Makes seven 6-oz. jars.*

4 large, sweet oranges (Valencia **or** other sweet variety)
1 medium lemon
8 cups water
8 cups granulated sugar
2 3/4 cups water
1/2 cup **Scottish Highland Liqueur**

Wash oranges and lemon. Trim ends and cut into quarters. Remove and discard all seeds. Thinly shred oranges and lemon by hand or with a shredding disc in food processor. (May be thinly sliced if preferred.) Pour shredded fruit and accumulated juice into a large glass or ceramic bowl(s), add 8 cups water. Cover and let stand 24 hours.

Remove any large pieces of improperly cut rind and fruit membrane. Pour shredded fruit and juice into an 8-quart or larger saucepan or canning kettle. Add remaining 2 3/4 cups water and bring mixture to a boil. Turn heat down so that a low boil is maintained. Stir in sugar and continue stirring gently until sugar has dissolved. Continue the low boil, stirring occasionally until marmalade is well reduced and forms a firm jelly when tested.

Begin to test the marmalade 30 minutes after the sugar has been added. Test either with a cooking thermometer (should reach 225° F) or with a spoon (marmalade should "sheet" when a small quanity is poured off the side of a spoon).

When the correct stage has been reached, turn off burner and stir in Scottish Highland liqueur. Let marmalade sit for 10 minutes before ladling into hot, sterilized jelly jars; seal.

FLAMING PINEAPPLE BOAT

A spectacular dish that may be served as a fruit salad or as a dessert. Serves 4 to 8.

1 fresh pineapple, cut in half lengthwise
1 can (8 oz.) mandarin orange sections, drained
2 bananas, peeled and sliced
1/2 cup maraschino cherries, well drained
1/3 cup orange **or Highland Marmalade**
1 Tbsp. **Pomegranate Liqueur**
1/4 cup **Orange** or **Royal Anne Cherry Liqueur**
1/4 cup sliced **or** slivered almonds
2 tsp. butter **or** margarine
3/4 cup shredded sweetened coconut
1/4 cup rum

Cut gently all the way around each pineapple half leaving a 1/2 " shell. Make two lengthwise cuts through the meat of the pine-apple (one on each side of the core), leaving three long sections in each half. Gently remove the two side sections first, then the center section, leaving an attractive shell for serving. Slice each long section into cubes and place in a large bowl. Cut out core, discard. Drain pineapple cubes before proceeding.

Place drained pineapple in large mixing bowl and add orange sections, cherries, bananas, marmalade and fruit liqueurs. Stir to combine gently and set aside to let flavors blend.

Sauté almonds and butter in saucepan until lightly golden. Add almonds and coconut to fruit mixture; stir in gently. Divide mixture evenly between pineapple shells. Arrange for serving. Place on baking sheets and heat fruit boats in a 325° F oven for 25 minutes or until warm throughout. Place on serving dish.

Just before serving, heat rum slightly in saucepan or microwave. Pour rum over boats; light quickly. Allow flames to die out before serving.

Note: May also be served cold. Don't heat or flame. Chill 2 hours.

FRUIT SALAD ADVOCAAT

*An easy and creamy salad. Serve for breakfast, brunch, lunch or as a dessert. Great idea: substitute **Advocaat Liqueur** for cream or half and half in your favorite fruit salad dressing for a taste surprise. Recipe serves 4.*

1 qt. prepared fresh mixed fruit, sliced **or** cubed
1/2 cup **Advocaat Liqueur**
1/2 to 1 cup whipped cream **or** topping (optional)

Combine all ingredients. Cover and chill for 1 hour or more before serving.

LAYERED FRUIT SALAD WITH LIQUEUR

*A dazzling and unique make-ahead salad. Use a glass bowl and layer by colors for maximum effect. Vary the fruits used with the seasons as well as the fruit liqueur flavors. Some of our favorite liqueurs may get you started, they are: **Blackberry, Japanese Plum, Orange, Raspberry** and **Strawberry**. This can also be served as dessert, if desired. Serves 8 to 10.*

2 bananas, sliced
1 pt. strawberries, sliced
2 oranges, sectioned
1 to 2 cups pitted cherries
2 apples **or** peaches **or** nectarines
1/4 honeydew melon **or** pears **or** berries
  lemon juice
  confectioners' sugar
1/2 cup fruit liqueur of choice

Place a layer of banana slices in a glass bowl. Lightly sprinkle with lemon juice, then cover with confectioners' sugar. Repeat in layers of fruit ending with sugar. Pour liqueur over all; cover and chill for 24 hours for best flavor.

119

INTERNATIONAL CHEESE SOUP

*We paired Swiss cheese with Greek **Ouzo** and were rewarded with a hearty yet subtly flavored soup. A special bread and green salad served with this main dish soup makes a memorable meal. Makes 10 cups.*

8 medium potatoes, peeled and diced
2 Tbsp. butter **or** margarine
2 medium onions, chopped
3 cups chicken broth
2 cups grated Swiss cheese
3 cups milk
1 Tbsp. **Ouzo Liqueur**
    chopped chives **or** croutons, as garnish

Place potatoes into a large soup pot. Cover with water and set aside while preparing onions. In a medium skillet, melt butter. Add onions and sauté until limp and transparent. Remove from heat.

Drain potatoes into a colander, discarding water. Return potatoes to pot and add chicken broth. Bring to a boil, lower heat and simmer, covered, until potatoes are soft. Remove from heat; stir in onions. Cool to lukewarm.

Using a blender or food processor, purée 2 cups of the potato mixture at a time until creamy and smooth. Repeat until all has been processed. Return to soup pot; add cheese and milk. Heat gently over medium-low heat, stirring often until cheese has melted and desired serving temperature is reached. (Do not allow soup to boil.)

Just before serving, remove from heat and stir in Ouzo. Garnish with croutons or chopped chives as desired.

COOKING WITH LIQUEURS
Hints and Tips

- **Herbal liqueurs** usually have strong flavors and should be used sparingly in food or cocktail recipes.

- A special seafood butter sauce can be made by combining melted butter and a dash or two of **Anisette Liqueur**.

- Use liqueurs much as you would extracts. Substitute a couple of tablespoons of **Crème de Menthe** or **Coffee** or **Orange Liqueur** for some of the water in your next chocolate cake for a surprising change.

- Pour a favorite fruit liqueur over a grapefruit half for a special treat.

- The easiest sundae of all: vanilla ice cream and your favorite liqueur. Also good topped with liqueured fruits and liqueur.

- To flambé a dish with a liqueur, warm the liqueur gently for one minute in the pan then ignite it carefully with a match. Or warm in the microwave. Place 1/3 cup liqueur in glass measuring cup and microwave on **HIGH (100%)** power 15 seconds.

- Add a can of drained mandarin oranges to any **Orange Liqueur** after the first straining. Age and strain as directed. Save oranges and top a cheese cake with fruit and drizzled liqueur.

- Add a couple of tablespoons of **Apple Liqueur** to your next apple, apple-berry, mince, quince or raisin pie for great flavor.

- Baste your next roast turkey with an **Orange** or **Cranberry Liqueur** for unique flavor.

- **Orange Liqueurs** are especially versatile for cooking. Drizzle over fruits for a special fruit cup or light dessert.

- **Herbal liqueurs** have historically been used for medicinal purposes. A tablespoon or two in fruit juice or hot tea or in a small liqueur glass to sip are common dosages.

INDEX

124

Main & Side Dishes/Meats

Preserves & Sauces

Soups & Salads

Book Order Form

Culinary Arts Ltd.
P.O. Box 2157, Lake Oswego, OR. 97035
(503) 639-4549 Fax (503) 620-4933

*Books are available at your favorite store
or by mail from Culinary Arts Ltd.*

___ CLASSIC LIQUEURS: The Art of Making &
Cooking with Liqueurs by Long & Kibbey
ISBN 0-914667-11-4 $8.95

___ THE BEST OF SCANFEST: An Authentic Treasury
of Scandinavian Recipes & Proverbs
Edited by Cheryl Long
ISBN 0-914667-13-0 $14.95

___ EASY MICROWAVE PRESERVING: The
Shortcut Way to Preserve Your Favorite Foods
by Fischborn & Long
ISBN 1-56440-016-6 $10.95

___ GOURMET MUSTARDS: How to Make and Cook
With Them by Helene Sawyer
ISBN 0-914667-07-6 $7.95

___ GOURMET VINEGARS: How To Make and Cook
With Them by Marsha Peters Johnson
ISBN 0-914667-10-6 $5.95

___ HAPPY BIRTHDAY: A Guide to Special
Parties for Children by Smith & King
ISBN 0-9610988-0-5 $9.95

___ Send FREE book & label catalog

For each address order please include:

Shipping and handling charge:

U.S. : $2.00 Book rate mail **or** $3.00 UPS/Priority Mail
Canada: $3.00 Book mail only

(A street address, not a P.O. Box is needed for UPS orders.)

Enclose check or complete for Visa or Mastercard:

Card #: _____ Exp. date: _____

Signature: _____

Ship To:

Name: _____

Address: _____

City/State: _____

Zip: _____ Phone: _____

To protect book, please photocopy order form.

*Our books are treasure-troves of information and
ideas but your satisfaction is priceless.
Your comments are invited.*